William Henry Green

Old Testament Canon and Philology

A Syllabus of Prof. Green's Lectures

William Henry Green

Old Testament Canon and Philology
A Syllabus of Prof. Green's Lectures

ISBN/EAN: 9783337169268

Printed in Europe, USA, Canada, Australia, Japan

Cover: Foto ©Lupo / pixelio.de

More available books at **www.hansebooks.com**

OLD TESTAMENT
Canon and Philology.

A SYLLABUS

OF

Prof. Wm. Henry Green's Lectures.

PRINTED—NOT PUBLISHED—EXCLUSIVELY FOR THE
USE OF THE STUDENTS OF THE

JUNIOR CLASS IN PRINCETON SEMINARY.

[PREPARED BY THE CLASS OF '80.]

PRINCETON:
PRESS PRINTING ESTABLISHMENT,
1878.

PREFATORY REMARKS.

It is hoped that all due allowance will be made for the various inaccuracies and defects in these notes. They are taken from the notes of a student of the Seminary who was here several years ago, and have been corrected or improved as they seemed to require. The abbreviations and the conciseness of statement are such as are usual in taking notes, and the labor of correcting proofs has been performed at odd moments in the midst of more essential duties. The Syllabus is offered to the Class under the conviction that they will not find in them a help to negligence of duty, but an assistance to reaching a higher and more efficient standard of scholarship.

S. R. H.

Introduction to Old Testament.

Lecture I.

O. T. consists of a number of separate books or treatises by different authors over a long period of time. Hence the necessity for studying the canon. *Canon*, κανών, any straight rod; then one used in measuring, as a carpenter's rule; then any rule to fix, regulate and determine other things. We speak of canons of Rhetoric, of Grammar. " Canons "=Standard authors. Also " that which fixes anything "—hence the Alexandrian Grammarians applied the word to the classics—thus in Gal. 6: 16; "according to this rule," τω κανόνι—So in 2 Cor. 10: 13. In the Fathers we find the words, canon of the church, canon of faith, and of the truth, &c.,—the *body of Christian doctrine*—this last expression was first found in Irenæus. As applied to *Scriptures*—*inspired rule of faith and practice*. This the modern use. The Old Testament canon consists of those books containing the rule of faith and practice given by God *prior to the coming of Christ;* not merely the list of books—this is a secondary and derivative sense.

Two things necessary to make a book canonical—1. Its *authorship;* by inspired men. 2. Its *design;* given to church as part of her permanent rule of faith.

The first is not all, all writings by inspired men are not *canonical*—See 1 Kings 4: 32. "Songs by Solomon" 1005; all lost; he also spake much on Natural History. &c. It does not follow that all his utterances were inspired, nor that every inspired prediction was intended to form part of the canon. So also as to the writings of Nathan, Ahija. Much that the prophets spoke was intended only for the existing generation and has not been kept; was intended only for a particular age or nation.

The historical books on which the books of Chronicles are founded are not in existence and never were in the canon. Decrees of Councils have value as being the concurrent testimony of many from a great region, thus giving precision, &c.

But no book ever in the canon has been lost.

The church has no authority to *decide* what *should be* in the canon—it is merely the *custodian and witness, to keep and testify to it*. Romanists hold the former doctrine. Romanists say the authority of Scripture is based on the authority of the church, as we have to go to the church of old to find out the canon. But the church has no existence without the Scriptures.

Two ways to study it.
(1) Historically.
(2) Theologically, to determine if correct on theological grounds.

Our inquiry is purely historical. What books have been given to, and from the beginning received by, the church as the canon?

Greater difficulties in Old Test. 1. Great antiquity, and absence of contemporaneous testimony. In N. T. each book is distinctly marked as to authorship—can be referred clearly to an inspired author. But in O. T. many books cannot be traced to their authors. 2. Entire *Christian* world is agreed about N. T. canon: not so with the O. T. canon. Romanists.

Advantages for O. T. canon. N. Test. has borne inspired witness to the other.

Inquire into 1. the HISTORY OF THE FORMATION into one volume, and 2. the EXTENT of O. T. canon, to identify the books which have been and ought to be in it. This second inquiry has three distinct though intimately related divisions; (1) the canon among the Jews, (2) the canon as recognized by Christ and his disciples, and (3) that recognized by the Christian church.

(1.) Presumptive argument, *a priori*. We may naturally expect that God would guard His revelation: that the people would do so; that if God would reveal His will for the permanent instruction of his people, He would take measures to preserve and safely transmit it: and also that the people to whom He communicated it would jealously guard it.

(2.) Argument from *analogy*, from heathen antiquity. The Romans had their Sibylline books, the Egyptians theirs, deposited with priests; the Babylonians, Phenicians, Greeks had sacred books and guarded them so.

(3.) Historical argument. But we are explicitly informed that such was the case with the Hebrews—Moses immediately after he had copied it, (for the last chapter of Deut., giving account of Moses' death, &c., must of course have been added by Joshua. He added also a description of the land—Josh. 24: 26,) commanded the Levites to put the book of the law in the side of the ark to be there for a witness—Deut. 31: 24–26; and that it should be read by the priests before all the people every seven years at the Feast of Tabernacles—Deut. 31: 9–13; the future king was required to transcribe the law—Deut. 17: 18. Joshua was required to have a copy and meditate upon it Josh. 1: 8—contains divine constitution and laws—the title-deed to Canaan, Josh. 24: 26. So other originals were guarded. See also 1 Sam. 10: 25; if even merely *national papers* were laid before the Lord, surely care was taken of His word. See also 1 Chron. 25: 7. Many of the Psalms of David were committed to the chief musician, a priest in the house of the Lord; "those trained in songs of the Lord were 288"—1 Chron. 25: 7. Hence such writings were preserved.

No doubt when the temple was built, the original copy of the law was transferred to it. Not disproved by 1 Kings 8: 9, or by 2 Chron. 5: 10. In both these passages it says that nothing was in the ark except the two tables of stone.

This objection is stated by some of the early Fathers and the later Rabbins. They were doubtless conversant with the more *modern* Jewish custom of putting a copy of the law in the ark which they have in the synagogue. It was not put *in* the ark ever, but "alongside" or in the side of it. 2 Kings 22: 8, shows that the law was treasured up somewhere in the temple until Josiah's reign at least 33 years before the exile. When the temple was burned, it did not involve the loss of the law, even if we disbelieve the tradition that Jeremiah hid it, for it was still in the minds of the people; and was read to them, Neh. 8: 1. Each king was required to have a copy, 2 Kings 11: 12. When Joash was crowned, Jehoiada, high-priest, gave him " the testimony."

There is a presumption that the rest of Scripture was preserved; if the people preserved the law of God, they would naturally preserve also what God spake through the prophets. And the people must have had many copies. Synagogues perhaps formed at captivity or later, but meetings were certainly held to read the law, Isa. 8: 16. " Bind up the testimony; seal the law among my disciples."

Isa. 8: 20—" To the law and to the testimony:" 1 Psalm.

These considerations prove the preservation of the *law of Moses* at least. The incorporation of the other inspired books is proved by independent hints only. We have evidence of this in the frequent allusions by succeeding prophets to their predecessors in recognition of their authorship and canonicity. The Proverbs not all written at one time and in their present form, but Prov. 25: 1, must mean inspired men in reign of Hezekiah completed them by making selections from extant writings of Solomon. " I, Daniel, understood by THE books, &c." Dan. 9: 2. Isa. 34:16 "Seek ye out *the book of the Lord* and read." THE " Books "—a definite and well-known collection, complete including Jeremiah his contemporary, Zech. 1: 4; 7: 12. " Lest they should hear the law, and the words which the Lord of hosts hath sent in His Spirit by the former prophets." After the exile, the law and the prophets are classed together as of like authority. Soon after the exile about 400 B. C. prophets and canon ceased with Malachi. Next proof, over 200 years later, 130 B. C. in prologue to the apocryphal book of Syrach or Ecclesiasticus—speaks of O. T. books as if collected and arranged in three divisions—when and by whom not stated by the author, but some time before even his grandfather's day, " studying the law and the prophets and the rest of the books."

Josephus, priest, born A. D. 37, says " there continued to be additions to O. T. till Artaxerxes of Persia (Esther), and then the exact succession of prophets ceased—and hence though books were still written, they were not of like authority, and none were so bold as to add to or take from 'the canon.' "

After this only legends and conjectures till time of Cyril—in relation to the process by which and the time when and by whom collected. (The time when and by whom they were collected in one volume does not affect their authority: they have as much when separate.) It is supposed Ezra put them in their present form. Evidence of this. 1. Legends aid. 2. Esdras—close 1st century, A.D., in chap. 14: 21, says the law was burned when the temple was, but Ezra by divine inspiration restored it, and in 40 days dictated 94 books, [ethiopic version (best) says—94 books, vulgate 204]—of which 24 to be written and for general circulation (the canon), and the rest oral, 70, only for the wise.

Same legend in early Christian fathers, Clemens Alexandrinus, Irenæus, Tertullian. They merely say Scriptures were lost and Ezra enabled to restore them without the loss of a single word or letter. But no credence should be given this, except so far as that Ezra did take a prominent part in collecting and editing the books after the exile. A tradition arose through Elias Leviter, a Rabbi of great eminence, about the time of the reformation, that Ezra and the Great Synagogue of 120 men collected the canon. No foundation for this except an obscure passage in the Talmud. 2nd Book of Maccabees says Nehemiah gathered the Acts of the Kings and prophets,—i. e., historical and prophetic books; the writings of David,—i. e., Psalms; and the Epistles of the kings concerning holy gifts [=letters of kings of Persia (decrees) which are preserved in Ezra,] and tries to say when and by whom different books were introduced into the canon, and then says Great Synagogue introduced books written outside of Palestine, viz., Ezekiel, Daniel and the 12 Minor Prophets—not clear. Great Synagogue =a body of men associated with *Ezra* and *Nehemiah* in over-sight of the spiritual affairs of the nation.

If any weight is to be given to the traditions it is only that Ezra and Nehemiah and perhaps others finally gathered them into one volume, and perhaps aided in multiplying and circulating them. This is probable from the following independent considerations, derived from the Scriptures themselves.

I. Ezra was a "*scribe*," " a ready scribe in the law of Moses"—" a scribe of the law of the God of heaven," &c. Known so before he went up from the Captivity. He was the first of that long list of scribes so prominent in after times, as custodians and servitors of the sacred text.— Nehemiah 8 : 4—12 : 26 and 36—Ezra, 7 : 6, 11, 12.

II. The period succeeding the exile was one in which there was great necessity and zeal for gathering and treasuring all the sacred relics, institutions, &c. Ezra engaged in restoring temple services, &c.

III. Order of prophets ceased with Malachi, who was contemporary with Nehemiah and Ezra: naturally gave rise to desire to collect the books.

IV. The succeeding period was conscious that prophecy had ceased. I. Maccabees, 4 : 46 ; 14 : 4 ; speaks of perplexity from want of a prophet—and decision of difficult questions, if a prophet should arise.

V. Statement of Josephus, no "*additions*, and no change" from time of Artaxerxes, ∴ not only written but collected by that time.

VI. II. Maccabees, 2 : 14, says of Judas Maccabeus : that he was " restoring the things lost during persecution : " means this probably—war with Antiochus Epiphanes, in his efforts to destroy the Jewish nation and religion. "*R*egathered all books lost by reason of the war and they remain with us :" this implies a previous gathering.

Recommend—Alexander on Canon (see evidences)— Canon Wordsworth, on Inspiration of the Scriptures. *Bishop Cosin's Scholastical History of the canon.* Apocrypha. Dr. Thornwell: arguments of Romanists discussed and refuted. Smith's Dictionary : Kitto on the canon. Also Canon Westcott on the Bible in the church.

The conclusion of all this is that the foundation of the Jewish canon was laid by Moses himself; that Joshua

was added, and perhaps others as written ; that the books were gathered by Nehemiah and Ezra shortly after the return from exile ; and the last book, written in the time of Nehemiah, was immediately added.

LECTURE II.

I. Extent of the Jewish Canon.

Of what books *precisely :* determine and identify the books.

Jews are now all agreed, and the unanimity exists as far back as we can trace.

Talmud, at least before 5th century—gives a catalogue of them in three classes—Law, Prophets and Kethuvim, otherwise called Hagiographa, *Ἁγιογραφη,*—sacred *writings* (Kathabh to write). Just the books we find in our Bibles are given here—24 books, according to the number of Greek letters, Samuel, Chronicles and Kings being each one book, the "twelve minor prophets" one, and "Nehemiah and Ezra" being in one.

Josephus—Born A. D. 37—priest, lived in Jerusalem, a Pharisee. Had therefore a good opportunity of knowing: in discussion against Appian only gives their number, not their names, and describes them.

He gives only 22 books, the number of Hebrew letters, attaching Ruth to Judges, and Lamentations to Jeremiah. This frequently done. Three classes.
 I. 5 Books by Moses.
 II. 13 " by Prophets.
 III. 4 " of Hymns to God and precepts for the conduct of human life.
 I. Same as usual.
 III. *Psalms, Proverbs, Ecclesiastes,* and *Song of Solomon.*
 II. Historical and Prophetical Books—Joshua, Judges and Ruth, Samuel, Kings, Chronicles, Ezra, Nehemiah, Esther, Job, Isaiah, Jeremiah and Lamentations, Ezekiel, Daniel, Minor Prophets.
 Can prove it also from his own works. Job and the three books of Solomon only are not quoted, as not relating to

the line of his history: but these are needed to make up his number, 22. Josephus nowhere quotes or makes use of any one of the apocryphal books.

We might prove it also by early Christian fathers. Find it later in account of canon as received in Christian church.

General argument. The canon could not have been corrupted before close of O T., for a succession of inspired men, the prophets, would most certainly have exposed it. Since then the extreme reverence in which it has been held by the Jews would not permit it; not to speak of the fact that an authentic copy was kept in the temple after the exile also. Josephus says—"How firmly we give credit to these books is evidenced by what we do, for we willingly suffer and die for them, and none are so bold as to add or take therefrom."

As to its safe handing down, even the Romanists admit it. But does it constitute *all?* Romanists say there are " *two* canons—one restricted, the other enlarged, Protocanonical and Deuterocanonical, of like authority."

Of the latter 7 are entire and there are parts of two others—Tobit, Judith, Wisdom, Ecclesiasticus or Cyrach, Barak, 1st and 2nd Maccabees: with chapters added to Esther and Daniel. "First canon earlier, 2nd later—no difference in authority and inspiration." Some distinguished Romanists say they " differ in grade of authority, though both inspired." But this is absurd—gives up the point: and they mean it.

In favour of 2nd canon they say that the canon being closed at the time of Malachi, all inspired books of a later date have to be put in a second canon.

Skeptical writers. They say the limitation of 1st canon was simply a matter of time: and was only a collection of all early Jewish writers. But

1. This ignores the character claimed and accorded to them from the beginning. All Jewish authors, Barak, Josephus, Philo, N. T. writers say they were from God.

2. The O. T. did *not* in fact contain all the extant writings. Chronicles, one of the latest O. T. books, mentions several histories and works as extant, viz., Nathan, Gad, Ahija, Iddo, &c. They are not *now* known in the

…any go after mass.
Cyrus ou was prior to,
tin with Josephine
?.. since artex.
'examination were

not positively prove
a collected, but twas
at that time
positively states. …
…was xxx… not artex.
mistakes do not destroy
it.

canon because *not in the canon then and not jealously guarded since;* and not because they had perished at the time the canon was made up.

The apocryphal books are refused, not because after a certain date, but because *not inspired.* Josephus says after Artaxerxes, prophets ceased.

Some say Jewish canon was "limited by the language in which written, and Apocryphal books not admitted because written in *Greek.*" But apocryphal books were originally in *Hebrew.* See Jerome, Maccabees, Tobit and Cyrach.

Some say there were two separate canons among the Jews—that, though only one at Palestine, the Jews elsewhere, as the Alexandrian Jews, had two.

No authority for this statement. The *Samaritans*, a schismatical body, not belonging to the Jews, it is true, acknowledged only the books of Moses, but this was because the later books conflicted with their cherished views, and not because the Jews in general attached superior authority to the books. They had their temple at Mount Gerizim, and therefore refused to accept books which recommended Zion and Jerusalem. Also had much intercourse with the heathen around them.

Some say the *Sadducees* acknowledged only Moses. Mistake. Josephus says 22 books were accepted by the nation at large, and if so large and powerful a portion of the nation as the Sadducees had not received all, he would have certainly mentioned it. Had this been so, Christ (Math. 22) would rather have rebuked them for it, than have given way to it: his design in using it was that a reference to Exodus might show them that the doctrine of the resurrection pervaded the entire Scriptures.

Mystics, Therapeutæ, Essenes, &c., accepted the canon and merely added their own views thereto.

The *Jews of Alexandria did* have lax views of inspiration, but even if they had had two canons, their position among the Gentiles would make us distrust any novelty from such a quarter.

1. These Jews also were extremely desirous of keeping up intercourse with Jews of Palestine, and nothing

would so effectually prevent this as introducing two canons.

2. Translator of Cyrach speaks of the book which his grandfather used in Palestine, and which he himself used in Egypt, and makes no distinction between them.

3. Josephus in his treatise againts *Appian*, an eminent Jew of *Alexandria*, speaks of no difference.

4. Philo makes repeated incidental reference to O. T. books, all same as those given in Talmud, as inspired: no mention of Apocryphal books.

Defense of Apocryphal books.

I. " *The Apocryphal books are in the Septuagint.*" Ad *ignorantiam.* (1.) But origin and even design of Septuagint is obscure: perhaps merely literary: ∴ collect all for the Library. Tradition, that it was translated by Ptolemy Philadelphus, for his library. (2.) Not all prepared at one time, or by one body of translators. Internal evidence. Varied merit and ability of translation. (3.) Apocryphal books were probably attached as appendix, as relating to the same subject, and not to anything in profane history.

II. " Accepted by Fathers."—Consider this objection later.

III. "Jerome's expression that 'Tobit and Judith ranked among the 'Hagiographa'—and since this was not so at Palestine, must have been so at Alexandria." But the word Hagiographa must be here a corruption for Apocrypha, for Jerome elsewhere expressly denies that these books were in the Hagiographa.

LECTURE III.

The CHRISTIAN canon brings the most decisive argument, although the foregoing is conclusive.

II. The books recognized by the Lord and the apostles.

They recognized the same as the Jews. They never charged the Jews with altering the letter of the law. Proved, *Negatively.* They never charge the Jews with *corrupting* or *mutilating* the word of God, though our Lord says they made it void by their traditions and gave erroneous interpretations of it. He would have reproved any omission or insertion.

Proved, *Positively*. 1. *By express statements.* "Unto them were committed the oracles of God," Rom. 3 : 2.

2. *By general implication.* Appeal to the sacred writings of the Jews as a WHOLE as "Scriptures," &c. John 5 : 39 ; Matt. 22 : 29 ; John 10 : 35. Or to the *three*-fold *division*, Matt. 5 : 17 ; Luke 24 : the "Law, Prophets and Psalms," the latter for Hagiographa, part for the whole, or because of the prevailingly poetical character of the Hagiographa, because the Psalms especially testify of Christ.

3. By their abundant *citations* of it as the word of God—of the Holy Ghost—of inspired men. All the books are thus quoted except some minor prophets and it is hard to tell which definitely. Ezra, Nehemiah, Ecclesiastes, Esther, admitted not to be quoted.

Every such citation lends the sanction of insipation to the canonicity of the book thus quoted, and to the entire volume in which this book is found. Those not cited are so merely because there was no occasion for it. They do not profess to quote all : it is merely incidental, for the moment.

They take O. T. as found among the Jews and ascribe to it divine authority : a most decisive proof that it contained nothing more nor less than what it should.

Objection—"N. T. writers used the Septuagint version and therefore sanctioned all the books which it contained, including the Apocrypha."

Answer—1. They admittedly did *not* sanction its *inaccuracies* : no more did they sanction its *spurious additions*. 2. And there was no danger of their being misunderstood by the Jews around—∴ did not EXPRESSLY SAY they accepted only the genuine. 3. They *never* even quote from the *Apocrypha*—in regard to every passage said to be so quoted it can be proved (a) that there is no such resemblance, or (b) that the passage in the Apocrypha is itself conformed to an O. T. passage, and this is what is in reality quoted—or (c) even if so quoted it merely affords the historical proof of the quotation merely; the apostles quoted even from heathen poets, and yet they did not sanction them. (d) They make positive statements which exclude these books. (e) Even prominent Romanists themselves have felt that the apostles did not sanction these passages.

Last resort of Romanists. The O. T. canon thus sanctioned is the true one: Even Bellarmin (a Romish authority), acknowledges that none other are canonical. Hence, we come to—

III. Canon recognized by the *Christian church*.

Last argument for Apocrypha—"These books must be canonical because sanctioned by the early church."

Even if this were true, the church might have erred in this: it erred in doctrinal matters (though here we reject the development theory, that the canon grew with the church).

Meaning of some *terms* used.

Canonical books=books inspired of God, given to the church as her rule of faith.

Canonical books, loose sense,=books agreeing in general character with inspired books, *orthodox* books.

Apocrypha—ἀποκρυπτω — "Hidden." 1. Some say this refers to the obscurity which clouded their origin, Augustine, (quid origo non pariut) *as regards their being inspired.* Yet Samuel, Kings, &c., have not known authors. But Ecclesiasticus is known as written by Son of Cyrach. 2. The *contents* of the books, mysterious, as the Eleusinian mysteries: not allowed circulation, as the heathen books (called κρυπτα) which are intelligible only to the initiated. Hence=heathenish i. e. heretical esoteric writings. 3. In contrast with the Scriptures, which were read in public worship—which hence="*open*" books, the others "hidden"=Heb. g'nuvim—(But the Jews applied this word to obscure passages in the canon itself and to copies of the Scriptures too full of mistakes to be used in the Synagogue.)

Apocrypha, used by the Fathers in two sense.s 1. As we use the word,=books claiming inspiration and place in canon but which have it not. 2. Books of pernicious character or forged to sustain heresies. According to

explanation. Ch. [illegible] only [illegible]
∴ PS. instead of [illegible]

2 Ch say [illegible] begin [illegible]
PS refer [illegible] because 1st Pt
or ,, , relating

(2) smith aff [illegible] Sol. Eccl. H[illegible]
,, not of [illegible], [illegible] cause [illegible]
acts other vols are not [illegible]

the latter sense, there were three classes of books. (a) *Canonical* or inspired. (b) *Ecclesiastical*, i. e. approved by the church for reading, or orthodox=our Apocrypha where "canonical" is used in its looser sense. (c) *Apocryphal*, books of evil tendency.

How are we to tell which the church did admit? 1. By catalogues. 2. By early versions. 3. By readings in public worship. 4. By quotations in the Fathers.

Catalogues of the sacred books—great authority—given 1. by the *Fathers:* 2. by *Councils*, valuable (a) as testimony of many fathers collected from a great extent of country. (b) Best, for they used more precise language.

Mélito—Bishop of *Sardis* (the church mentioned in Revelation)—oldest catalogue—A. D. 160—only one of 2nd century. He travelled to Judæa and inquired carefully. He opposes all but those in the Hebrew volume. Gives their names, not their number. 1. Abundant testimony elsewhere, and 2. this is not a question of dispute. Romanists admit this. Adds the words ἡ καὶ σοφία after Proverbs; ∴ Romanists say it means the Apocryphal book of *Wisdom*. But the real meaning (ἡ καὶ not καὶ ἡ) is " which is also wisdom," referring to Proverbs. *Lamentations* not mentioned : probably included under Jeremiah. *Ruth*, with Judges. So Nehemiah, probably included under ~~Esdras~~. Esther not mentioned—begins in Septuagint with an Apocryphal section and ∴ Esther joined to Jeremiah ; or Melito inadvertently rejected the whole of it, or fault of transcriber, or included in another book.

Justin Martyr. 2nd century, died 164 A. D. Born in Palestine, after conversion lived in Rome. No regular catalogue. Quotes frequently, but never from Apocrypha. In his controvery with Trypho, a Jew in Ephesus, he does not refer to Apocrypha nor accuse the Jews of rejecting inspired works, as he would naturally have done had he believed those books inspired.

Syriac Peshito, 2nd century, only included canonical books.

Origen—Greek Father—3rd century—most learned of Greek Fathers. Educated at Alexandria. Died at Tyre, 70 years of age. His catalogue gives 22 books. as preserved by Eusebius in his Ecclesiastical History, the same as Josephus, and then says—"and *apart* from these are books of Maccabees." Minor prophets omitted, but inadvertently, and not by Origen himself, for they are found in every other catalogue, and are necessary to complete the 22, (he says 22, and names only 21)—∴ fault of the transcriber. The old Latin translation by Ruffin gives it.

Under Jeremiah he includes Lamentations and "*Epistle of Jeremiah.*" This must be either the epistle to the captives at Babylon, Jer. 29; or an Apocryphal epistle given in the Vulgate as the last chapter of Baruch. Probable that he was *misled*, for Origen follows the Hebrew canon *professedly*, and this certainly never contained it.

Tertullian.—3rd century—no catalogue—speaks of 24 books as in Talmud. Tertullian, oldest of Latin fathers whose works have been preserved to us, thinks the number 24 refers to the 24 beasts around the throne, and the 24 elders, in Revelation. ∴ In 2nd and 3rd centuries, we have Melito and the Syriac from the Eastern church; Origen from Greek church; Tertullian from Latin church.

Fourth Century.—Corroborated from all parts of church. Council of Laodicea. Representatives from Asia.

Greek Writers. { Athanasius—Bishop of Alexandria.
Cyril— " Jerusalem.
Epiphanius— " City of Salamine, in Cyprus
Amphilochius—" Iconium.
Gregory of Nazianzus— " Constantinople.

Basil *the Great* of Cappadocia, and *Chrysostom* of Constantinople give no formal catalogues but equivalent statements—the former says the number was 22: the latter says all the books of O. T. were written in Hebrew —∴ he followed the Jewish canon.

Latin Writers. { Hilary—Bishop of Poitiers.
Ruffinus— " of Aquileia, in Italy.
Jerome—Monk of Palestine, (most learned man of his time, born in Dalmatia.)

Two, those of *Athanasius* and *Epiphanius*, omitted *Esther*—explained as under Melito. Athanasius even puts

it among Apocrypha, but for the same reason. There is abundant proof of its canonicity: the only difficulty is to ascertain clearly how this difference happened. They reject whole of Esther, because burdened with spurious chapters. Hilary says "Jeremiah and his epistle"—(see Origen)— Athanasius, Cyril and Council of Laodicea speak of "Jeremiah, Baruch and the epistle," but Baruch may = part of genuine Jeremiah, (29 chap.) which speaks of Baruch—may be the Apocryphal book of Baruch, which contains this epistle.

Later catalogues have not book of *Baruch* in Apocrypha, which Rome says is canonical.

With these exceptions all sustain the Protestant canon. The catalogues of the first four centuries uniting with strict canon. Rome says they give the Jewish canon, and not the larger Christian canon—mere evasion. They give the Jewish because the Christian is the same as this.

Again they say they are excusable for the church had given no decision yet. But the church can't *decide* this: all we want is testimony.

ROMANIST OBJECTIONS.

At the close of the fourth century Augustine (good theologian, poor critic)—and the councils of Hippo and Carthage, added most of the books which are now in Romish canon—

(I.) But *not exactly same.* Baruch not in any—and first Esdras=Nehemiah and Ezra, and they contain a book of Esdras (2nd of Vulgate, 1st of English apocrypha) which Rome does not recognize as inspired.

(II.) These are not=three independent witnesses. Augustine was bishop of Hippo near Carthage and his influence and views probably determined the decisions of the two Councils.

(III.) They would not reasonably differ so greatly from what was held in all the rest of the church, and in Carthage itself at an earlier date.

(IV.) The preface and conclusion of the catalogues shows they were meant to include not merely *inspired* works, but also orthodox, edifying ones. Augustine advises a distinction—that those received by all the churches should be preferred to those received by fewer, and among the latter preference should be given to most important or influential churches. He certainly would not have made such a distinction among *inspired* books. Used "canonical" as referring to good, profitable, edifying books.

(V.) He elsewhere says "the Jews had no prophet after Malachi until the father of John the Baptist." And yet the Apocrypha was written in that interval. And he says "all the books of O. T. were with the Jews, who=librarians of the church." But the Apocrypha was rejected and also Judith. And says "the Jews don't receive Maccabees as they do the law, the prophets, and the Psalms, but it is received by the church as books good to be read, especially Maccabees, who suffered persecution so much for the faith." A sect called Circumcelliones allowing suicide appealed to the case of Drasis in 2nd Maccabees. To these persons Augustine replies "they are in great straits for authorities, having only this book, one which neither Jews, nor Christ, nor the Apostles sanctioned as they did the prophets and Psalms," and "which the church receives only as the history of men who suffered for God." And says "they are to be read *soberly* and with caution, only that which is sound being received." Self-murder, though approved in Maccabees, is not right. Maccabees as "canonical," means as approved by church for private and public reading. "What is not in the canon of the Jews cannot be received with so much confidence against opposers." *council*

(VI.) There is a presumption that the church at Carthage did not design to cut itself off from rest of the church, for it proposed to submit this canon to the judgment of Boniface, Bishop of Rome.

Question whether this catalogue is authentic and among the decrees of the church.

(VII.) Tertullian, a lawyer of Carthage, in preceding century, and Primazius and Junilius in fifth century, add their testimony.

Primazius—Bishop of Africa later—admits only 24 books.

Junilius distinguishes among the "divine" books—some of perfect, some of medium, some of no authority.

Hence Carthage had not the canon, in its wide sense,—in strict sense, the same.

Hence by *all* the "canon" was used in its looser sense.

Thus we see there was no disagreement in the first four centuries, if the word "canon" be used in the strict sense. Same canon now.

LECTURE IV.

We have seen that all the catalogues except *three* sustain *our* canon; and that they do so without ambiguity. And that these *three* have no more weight than *one*; and that they do not in reality disagree from the other, but merely use the word *canon* in the loose sense. But even if this be not so, it is enough to condemn the Apocrypha that it is not in any catalogue before the 4th century.

Parallel of O. and N. T. Canon. To neutralize this the Romanists bring up the Antelegomena, disputed books of the N. T. which were not generally received until the 4th century, but which we all hold canonical now. But the cases are not similar. The Antelegomena consists of a few small books which required time to become generally known; they were gladly accepted where *first known*, and gradually spread. But the Apocrypha (1) were *never* so accepted where first known; (2) where so adopted, it was without critical investigation; (3.) were classed with O. T. *loosely*; (4.) and even in this lax sense were not *universally* received. N. T. was.

Greek Church.—History of the Canon after the 4th Century. Followed the Council of Laodicea, against the Apocrypha without a dissenting voice.

Latin Church.—Division. Many were influenced by Augustine's great learning; as well as influenced by the growing custom of public reading; others follow Jerome (strict), but the greater number, especially of the intelligent, favored only the strict canon. *Catalogues* for the large canon in all this time, only two or three.

Gregory VIII., the Great, A. D. 600, First Bishop of Rome, quoting from Maccabees, speaks of them as "not canonical, but yet published for the edification of the church." Councils of Trent, France, England, &c., agree with strict canon. All are considered authorities.

There are few genuine authorities favoring Augustine's catalogue.

In the 16th century, Cardinal Ximenes, Archbishop of Toledo, (author of Complutensian Polyglot,) says in the preface, as his dedication to Pope Leo, and approved by him, "These books of the Apocryphal O. T. (given in Greek only) were not in the canon, and were received by the church rather for edification than for doctrine."

Cardinal Cagetan, at Rome, an eminent theologian, who would have been Pope, had he lived after Clement X., defended the strict canon only ten years before the Council of Trent.

The Prologue of Jerome, *defending the strict canon*, is always in the preface to the Romish Bible.

Council of Trent—ecumenical and binding in its decrees—8th April, 1546, adopted the looser canon as inspired: "The Apocrypha is to be received with equal veneration with the other O. T. books," and decreed anathema on those who rejected it. This is really the *first time* it was ever decreed that these books were on a par with the inspired word of God; or that those of contrary views should be anathema. The decision was owing not to thorough investigation, but to the fact that at that time many of the "lessons" of the church were from the Apocrypha, and to the desire to make an issue with the Protestants. There was *much* and earnest dissent in the council even then.

Other Romanist Arguments for Apocrypha, besides the early catalogues:

I. Contained in *early versions*. 1
II. Read in public *worship* early. 2
III. Quoted by *early Fathers* as of *Divine authority*. 3

Prelim. Remark—The whole church was united for the strict canon. Even if undue value was placed upon the Apocrypha in certain places, even if some have expressed themselves thoughtlessly, incautiously, on the subject, yet the general opinion is against them.

I. *Objection* " contained in early versions."—Answer.
(1.) Apocrypha was not in all ancient versions. The *Syriac* Peshito, and the Latin version of *Jerome* did not have them. The latter is the foundation for the Vulgate, which took the *Apocrypha*, however, from an earlier Latin version—the *Itala*.

(2.) Though in the *Septuagint*, it was there as a mere appendage, not as equal to the rest in authority, because the Alexandrian Jews, *among* whom and *for* whom the translation was made, did not so receive the Apocrypha; other early versions made from the Septuagint were copied in the Apocrypha as an *integral part*.

(3.) The Romish argument inverts the real order of facts and makes the effect the cause, saying it was in early versions because it was inspired, whereas it was considered inspired by them merely because it was in ancient versions. There was a great dearth of religious books, and therefore these were more naturally classed with Bible, and bound with it, to " kill two birds with one stone " in their circulation. For most early Fathers did not understand Hebrew; it was therefore translated from the Greek versions.

(4.) From *analogy* of modern versions. It might have been included in the early versions without being considered inspired. See Luther's version—King James' version.

(5.) Their argument, if valid, proves *too much*. They reject as uncanonical, 3rd Esdras and 3rd Maccabees, and the Prayer of Manasseh, which are in early versions. The Ethiopic version contains even more, as the book of Enoch.

II. *Objection*—" Read in public worship in same manner as canonical books, and therefore equal."

(1.) The fact is admitted but the argument from it is unsound; everything turns on the *intention* with which *they* read it; must first show this before the argument is of any weight.

(2.) From analogy. Church of England shows that its being read in churches and being canonical, are not the same thing necessarily. " Read on festival days and not on the Sabbath."

(3.) That the early church in reading these books thus did not thereby esteem them canonical, appears from express testimony. *Jerome*—"Read for instruction, but not to prove any doctrine." Very explicit. *Ruffin* says, "there are other books not canonical, but are called Ecclesiastical, as Wisdom of Solomon, or Cyrach or Ecclesiasticus. To be read in the churches, but not for authority in faith." *Athanasius*—"Contains not indefinite, but determined and canonized books, but also others not canonical, but read by catechumens, as Wisdom, Cyrach, Judith, Tobit."

(4.) This argument also would prove too much, for many books were read which Rome herself does not esteem canonical.

III. *Objection*—"Quoted by Early Fathers in a way which shows they esteemed them inspired." The most plausible objection; but even if well-founded, we must take it cautiously in connection with *other* evidence But it is not a valid objection, however.

(1.) Ascertain whether the quotation alleged is really from the Apocrypha.

(2.) If so, whether it is quoted as from the inspired word of God.

I. *Fact* of being quoted? Answered.

First Century. In the Fathers of this century there are a few allusions to persons and things in the Apocrypha, and a few expressions like those in the Apocrypha, but no formal quotations from it. This shows merely that they were acquainted with the Apocrypha.

From the Second Century on. (a) Freely quoted. So are Homer, Virgil, &c. Shows only that they were known or contained something pertaining to the matter in hand. (b) The Apocrypha is mentioned with respect and reverence, and appealed to as *true*, but not as *inspired*.

II. *Manner* of quotation: There must be something in the mode of quotation showing it to have been regarded as inspired; of this there is no proof. Rome says they do so quote. (1.) "They make use of the same formulas in quoting from Apocrypha as in quoting from the other books." (2.) "They employ the same terms in speaking of the writers of these as in speaking of those of the other books."

Objection I. Formula—"It is written," the established phrase for "quoting" from the inspired word. They speak of Apocrypha as the Holy Scriptures, Divine Scriptures. But (1) although to us the word *Scripture*, from long and familiar usage suggests the *Bible*, yet its original import is general—*writings* (γραφη); and *sacred* scriptures—writings on sacred subjects. In other words, they merely meant Sacred Literature, in contrast with Profane Literature, using the loose sense of canonical.

(2.) That the phrases are used in this general sense or in the loose sense just mentioned, is shown by the fact that the same writers who *exclude* these books from the inspired word, yet cite them under these terms—Origen, Jerome, Athanasius. Origen quotes Tobit, Wisdom, &c., and speaks of them as the Divine word, and yet in his catalogue of the canon, leaves them out.

(3.) Such distinctions are made in the "divine books," &c., as to show that these terms *must* have been general. *Junilius* says " some divine books are of perfect authority, some of medium, some of no authority." *Cyprian* quotes from the Apocrypha as the *Scriptures*, and then tries to *establish the truth* of the quotation by referring to *Acts*, which he calls the "testimony of truth."

(4.) Analogy—The Homilies of the Church of England cite some books under the name of *Scriptures*, as the Book of Wisdom.

(5.) Their argument proves too much. Books are cited under this name by Augustine and others, which Romanists themselves do not admit and never have admitted, viz: the Apostolic Constitutions, the Book of Enoch, even the Sibylline Verses, &c.

II. Another class of quotations. Writers are called by titles proper only to inspired men, as prophets, etc., or the writings are attributed to some known inspired writers, as "the 5 Books of Solomon," viz: the three genuine ones, Wisdom, and Cyrach.

Answer—(1.) These expressions are in a loose, popular sense, so declared by Augustine, who says the two other books are attributed to Solomon (see above) and are so because of their similarity of style. So "Book of Daniel" does not assert that Daniel was the author, and so "Baruch and Jeremiah."

(2.) If we insist, however, on these points, they only prove that the Fathers were mistaken, for it can clearly be shown that many of the books so spoken of are not genuine.

(3.) The Fathers did *not* mean that they were the word of God, for they elsewhere expressly exclude them.

(4.) Analogy—Church of England calls Baruch " a prophet."

(5.) Proves too much—" argumentum ad hominem." So Rome cites 3rd and 4th Esdras under Ezra.

ERGO, the Apocrypha was excluded by the Jews, by our Lord and the Apostles, and by the Christian church generally, if not universally, until Council of Trent.

INTERNAL EVIDENCE.

Not *decisive* (e. g. Esther, Ruth, Ecclesiastes,) yet *aids* in settling the extent of the canon. Even Luther doubted the canonicity of the Epistle of James, because it seemed to contradict the apostle Paul. Historical evidence must decide historical questions. A book containing what is false in fact or doctrine or unworthy of God, is not inspired: Tobit and Judith so--are full of topographical and chronological mistakes.

TOBIT—1: 4-5. In the youth of Tobit the ten tribes revolted from Judah under Jeroboam. Hence he must have been 270 years old at the Assyrian captivity, at which time he was taken captive. But (14: 11) he was only 158 years old when he died.

His angels' visits, contrary to all analogy, are long continued; an angel journeying on foot with him 300 miles. The angel Raphael induces him to lie to Azarias and to call himself a captive of Naphtali—5: 12. 12: 15.

He teaches a doctrine nowhere else taught: of seven angels going in and out before God; borrowed from Persian superstition.

His absurdities. An evil spirit in love with a woman; can be driven away only by a smoking heart and the liver of a fish—6: 7-17. Says almsgiving can deliver from death and purge away all sin. 12: 9. 14: 10 and 11.

JUDITH—6: 10-11. The scene is laid in Bethuliah; no trace of it. The name means *virgin*. It is probably an allegory or romance.

There is no time possible for the events related; as the protracted peace of 80 years, &c. The march of Holofernes is decidedly zigzag. The book says it was in the reign of Nebuchadnezzar, king of Nineveh, (1: 1); but *Babylon* was his capital. That Joiakim was the contemporary high-priest; but there was no high-priest of this name till *after* the exile.

Judith's language and conduct is false and deceitful. Teaches the Jesuitical plea that "the end justifies the means." Even prays God to assist her in so doing. The crime of Simeon, condemned in Gen. 49: 5: is here praised. It is said to be a crime to break the ceremonial law even to *save life.* (11: 10.) Jesus taught otherwise.

LECTURE V.

Internal Evidence Against the Apocrypha.

(continued).

The Books of Wisdom and Cyrach or Ecclesiasticus, contain many excellent maxims, yet their morality is defective, and is based mainly on *expediency.* And the wisdom is less that of Solomon than of the late Alexandrian philosophers.

Wisdom 7: 25—The doctrines of Emanation from God, and (8: 19–20) pre-existence of the soul are taught, and that the world was created from preëxisting matter.

9: 15—That the material body is a weight upon the soul.

10: 15–20—Israel is represented as *righteous*, and all God's favors to it as a just *reward.* Even real miracles are spoken of in an exaggerated way, from mere love of the marvellous.

16: 20–21—It says the manna was agreeable to every taste, and tempered itself to every man's liking.

16th and 17th Chaps.—Plagues of Egypt are described with embellishments which are not warranted.

18: 24–25—False explanation of the high-priest's dress: virtue is ascribed to his *dress* which is due only to his mediatorial office.

10 : 4—Cain's murder of Abel is said to have caused the flood.

14 : 15—The account of the origin of idolatry, flimsy and untrue. " Owing to fathers making images of their deceased children." *No moral* cause is assigned, as by Paul, in Rom. 1 : 21–23.

7th Chap. and 9 : 7–8—Solomon said to be the author, yet the people are spoken of as being at the time under subjection to their enemies—15 : 14.

And it can be proved that it was originally written in *Greek.*

CYRACH OR ECCLESIASTICUS.—Many passages teaching justification by works.

3 : 30—Almsgiving atones for sin.

3 : 3 —Honoring parents atones for sin.

35 : 3 —And forsaking unrighteousness atones for sin.

12 : 26–28—Kindness to the wicked is prohibited.

33 : 26–28—Cruelty to slaves is allowed.

50 : 25–26—Hate towards Samaritans is also allowed. Exhortations to do right to gain the favor of men. Expediency substituted for right as the ground of obligation.

38 : 18—" Weep for the dead, lest thou be evil spoken of."

Chap. 7.—Carnal enjoyment taught, because life is brief.

45 : 15.—" Aaron priest, as long as the heavens stand."

BARUCH.—Said to have been written by Baruch, the helper of Jeremiah, yet originally in Greek, and quotes Nehemiah and Daniel, who lived later. Baruch is said to have gone to Babylon : did not if the real Baruch, but went to Egypt.

The Temple is spoken of as standing, and offerings were to be made in Jerusalem, though in Jeremiah's time it was in ashes.

Belshazzar is called the son of Nebuchadnezzar, though he was his *grandson.*

Speaks of sending vessels back by Jeremiah, (1 : 8) though this was not done till after the exile. See Ezra 1 : 7.

3 : 4—" God hears the prayers of the dead." (So also 2d Maccabees, 15 : 14 teaches.) Proof texts for Romanists.

The captivity according to Jeremiah, 70 years; Baruch's Epistle of Jeremiah says seven generations. Manifestly written later therefore, and as an explanation.

I. and II. MACCABEES.—I. Has many errors, historical and geographical, but is better than II., which abounds in fables and legends. In the latter, preservation of sacred fire; Jeremiah hiding the tabernacle and ark and altar of incense, in Mount Nebo, and the apparition which is said to have prevented the Emperor Heliodorus from invading the sanctity of the Temple. Justifies suicide; prayers for the dead.

The writer does not even claim inspiration—15 : 38–39. " Wrote according to his ability."

ESTHER.—The genuine Book of *Esther* only in Hebrew; the spurious additions only in Greek, and in the old Latin version. Jerome remarks as to the addition, that some writer undertook to add what might have been said. But it really breaks the connection, contradicts, and adds things improbable and evidently untrue. The Sophists did so often.

ADDITIONS TO DANIEL.—Three of them.

I. Prayer of the three children in the fiery furnace Devotional, but not adapted to the occasion or their situation, (verses 23–27) and contains unwarrantable assertions.

II. Story of Susannah—improbable.

III. Bel and the Dragon—absurd and ridiculous.

The Council of Trent, though few in members, and representing a limited territory, imposed the Apocrypha as inspired, in the face of all preceding authority, upon the whole Romish church, denouncing its anathema on all who presumed to reject it. Since then, of course, the line of witnesses in the Latin church, against the Apocrypha, has ceased. Yet some few object, and make a distinction between the Deuterocanonical (i. e. the Apocrypha) and the Protocanonical books—the former as of less authority and veneration. But this does not accord with the language of the Council of Trent, and there can be no degrees in such a matter.

Greek Church.

Favors the strict canon.

Cyril Leucar, 1631, Constantinople—address to the Council of Laodicea.

Dositheús, of Jerusalem, 1672, under Romish influence, sanctioned the Apocrypha.

Platon, of Moscow, approves of the authorized Russian catechism, and authorizes only the strict Jewish canon.

Protestant Church.

Has always been unanimous for the strict Hebrew canon as to its *inspiration*. The opinion about the *use* of the Apocrypha has been various, (none regarding it as inspired, but) some approving the "reading of it for instruction in life and manners, though not for doctrine" (Jerome.) Church of England :—the Westminster Confession says it is to be used no more than human writings.

The former of these views naturally led to keeping it in Bibles as an appendix; the latter banished it altogether from the volume. The antagonism culminated in the "Apocryphal controversy." The German branches of the British and Foreign Bible Society used Luther's version, containing the Aprocypha. In 1811, the Society resolved to require its auxiliaries to leave out the Apocrypha. Owing to opposition, the order was rescinded in 1814. In 1819 the Society allowed their auxiliaries to print the Catholic Bibles in Italian, Spanish and Portuguese Bibles and insert the Apocrypha with the inspired books indiscriminately—saying the Bible could not be distributed in those countries unless it were so. Much opposition, resulting in the compromise (1822) that they should use the money of the Society only to print the strict canon, the Apocrypha at private expense. Still many were dissatisfied. -In 1827 it was resolved by the Society that " no person or association circulating the Apocrypha should receive aid from the Society, and none but bound books should be issued." Strife renewed in Germany lately, some theologians entirely excluding the Apocrypha, some claiming a subordinate place for it owing to long ecclesiastical usage. But the usage grew up when books were scarce; now that books are plenty and accessible, it is not necessary to put the two together.

But the Apocrypha deserves to be carefully read, for its prominence in the controversy and because it has some intrinsic worth (especially I. Maccabees), and sheds much light on the canonical books, explains customs, &c.

The threefold division of Law, Prophets and Hagiographa or Kethuvim (writings.) This threefold classification is first referred to in the Prologue to Cyrach, where this division is mentioned twice. Five books are in the Law, eight in the Prophets, and eleven in the Hagiographa. For Josephus' division see previous lecture, page 9. He made it for his own use and purpose. See also Luke 24: 44.

Our Lord only singles out the book of Psalms from the Hagiographa as mainly Messianic; or else the Psalms, as being the leading book, first in order, and most important, is named to include the rest. So we speak of the Confession of Faith, and Book of Common Prayer. It is said they also bear internal evidence of gradual and successive formation.

"Law first; all given subsequently were afterwards gathered into a second volume, the Prophets, which was closed: a third collection was again made of ones which were not before known or discovered, and this is the third division or Kethuvim." Those who make this statement say it is confirmed by the fact that there are books in the third division which should have been in the second if they had been known. Daniel is not in the Prophets but in the third division. Kings in the second among Prophets; but Chronicles, which has precisely the same character, is in the third. Hence they say the formation into three classes was a process of time and discovery.

Reply—I. This view is based upon the idea that the collection of the canon was a purely literary rescue from destruction. But the books were *all* well known, and all the collectors had to do was to arrange them.

II. This theory of time, &c., does not account for the phenomenon. They say the book of the Prophets was closed. What is meant by this? Not so as long as any book remained; no sense in which it can be true.

III. The whole theory is in conflict with the facts: the Psalms, &c., were known when the collection of the Prophets was made, and the Psalms were used in temple-worship. Why not then in this division?

IV. There is an easy and satisfactory explanation. The Rabbins distinguished various grades of inspiration in the inspired writers. 1st. The Law, given to Moses face to face with God; 2nd. the Prophets, those written under the influence of the spirit of prophecy; 3rd. those written under the ordinary inspiration of the Holy Spirit. Some truth in this tradition. The ground is the official character of the authors.

1. Moses' functions were unique, the legislator.
2. Prophets *officially* such, class by themselves.
3. There were other inspired men not set apart specially, men exercising secular functions, as, David, Solomon, Daniel, Ezra, Nehemiah. The Chronicles were probably written by Ezra, the Kings by a Prophet; using the word in the proper official sense of the term.

∴ The classification regards not the contents but the authors.

Only one book, Lamentations, causes any embarrassment, according to this principle. The *prophecies* of Jeremiah are among the Prophets: and it is probable that Lamentations was originally also so included. It seems so from the enumerations of Josephus and of Origen, who give only 22 books, and Lamentations must then have been included under Jeremiah's prophecies. It was probably transferred afterward for liturgical purposes, or from its resemblance to the Psalms.

This division was in force in the time of Christ, Matth. 23:35. As if to take from the extremes of Scripture, as well as of time, Abel (in the first book) is mentioned, and Zacharias from (probably the last book of the O. T. written) II. Chronicles. Though this is not decisive.

Greek and Latin and English Bibles give a fourfold division.

1. Law—Pentateuch.
2. Historical Books.
3. Poetical "
4. Prophetical "

14

Athanasius divides into four Pentateuchs, covering all but two of the books, Ezra and Esther.
1. Moses' Books.
2. Five Historical Books.
3. Poetical Books—Job, Psalms, Proverbs, Ecclesiastes, Canticles.
4. Prophetical Books—Isaiah, Jeremiah, Ezekiel, Daniel, and the Minor Prophets.

Samaritans had 27—count double books as single. This corresponds with the Hebrew alphabet, 22 consonants, 5 double forms. This is according to Jerome and Epiphanius.

The number 33 has also been given, making with N. T. Books, 60 in all. This was done by counting the 12 Minor Prophets singly, and not as one. The number 60 was given a mystical sense, as referring to the 60 queens of Solomon. The English version of the O. T. numbers 39.

CEREMONIAL INSTITUTIONS OF MOSAIC LAW.

LECTURE I.

The Law of Moses as it relates to worship, may be divided into—

Sacred *Places*—Tabernacle.
" *Persons*—Priesthood.
" *Actions*—The Ritual.
" *Times*—The Calendar.

1. THE TABERNACLE.—Rectangular; 30 cubits long, 10 wide, 10 high—divided into 2 apartments by a richly wrought veil. 1. *Holy of Holies*—Innermost room; perfect cube; 10 cubits each way. 2. The *Holy Place*—Rectangle; 20 cubits long, 10 high and wide. This was separated from the court by another rail. 3. The *Court*—100 cubits long, 50 cubits wide, 5 cubits high. The people were admitted only to the court, in which stood the *Altar of Burnt Offering* and the *Laver*. The *Priests* were admitted into the Holy Place, in which were the *Altar of Incense*, the Golden Candlestick and the Table of Shew Bread. Into the Holy of Holies, containing the Ark and Mercy Seat, only the High Priest could go, and that once a year—on the great day of Atonement.

MEANING AND DESIGN.

Is there any special signification in the structure, apart from its uses? It might be that the ritual was the only significant portion, and everything else subsidiary to it. There must be *some* place for this ritual, also priests and set times. While it is true that the ritual was the most essential and important, to which the others are subsidiary, yet the latter had their signification. 1. This appears *first*, because the arrangement and plan of the structure are not determined by simple regard to convenience or adaptability of its uses. (a) The build-

(2) [illegible handwritten notes]

---

3 distinct Codes given to Jews
(1) Book of Covenant (Exodus 21–23)
(2) Levitical Code. (Ex 25—)
(3) Deuteronomy by Moses [illegible]

ing was not demanded to shelter the crowd of worshippers, for they were not really sheltered at all. The court was open to the sky. (b) The dimensions were out of proportion to its contents. (c) No purpose of convenience was answered by closing these from the light, nor (d) do we know why they were set toward the East.

Second Reason.—The minute and careful directions in the most trifling matters, e. g., the number of boards in the court, chords, loops, curtains, &c. This shows some further meaning in the thing itself. Nothing was left to human invention. All was prescribed by God. This shows its sacredness and heavenly origin, just as in Rev. 21 : 15; 11 : 1–2; also in *Ezekiel.* Rev. 11: 1–2—The court was not to be measured but given to the Gentiles. Measurements imply sacredness.

Third Reason.—Moses (Ex. 25 : 40; 26 : 30) was directed to make all things after the pattern shown him in the Mount.

What was the Symbolical Meaning? Various views:

I. The *Materialistic.*—Some say that it was modelled after the tents of earthly rulers, and was designed to be the abode of the divine monarch of Israel. There is a gross material sense of this view held by some, as though God had the same necessities and wants as men. This view is inconsistent with God's nature. To this we say: The plan does not correspond to a human tent. The seat or throne is set in a dark apartment; the candlestick in another room. The food is on the table, the fire on the altar, but no bed. Its being made after the pattern shown in the Mount, proves that it was not made after a human tent. Others who have held this general view, said it was an ideal structure for God, who had no need of shelter, but yet condescended to dwell in a tent. There is a measure of truth in this, but still it does not explain the structure.

II. *Cosmical Theory.*—They say the Tabernacle, &c., represents the Universe. The Tabernacle represented heaven, and the Court represented the earth.

Three Modifications of this View;

1. It represented the material heaven and earth. Philo, Josephus, some Christian Fathers, Talmud and

the Rabbins, held this. They held that the contents of the Tabernacle were celestial, and those in the Court terrestrial. The Seven Lamps represented the seven planets: Twelve Loaves=twelve signs of the Zodiac: Two Cherubim=the two hemispheres of the heavens, winged to denote constant motion. Four Materials of the Veil=the four elements. In the Court, the Laver=the sea. The Altar =the land. This view is false because (1) there is no intimation in Scripture that these objects were represented in the temple. (2) This would be a mere worship of nature, like the heathen who had these objects in their temples. (3) The very objects here supposed to be represented, are those which were forbidden to be represented by images and worshipped—Deut. 4:19; Ex. 20:4. This would seduce the people to idolatry by Divine appointment, the same thing that Manasseh was accused of doing—2 Kings 21:15. (4) The Tabernacle would thus contain none of the things we should expect to find there in connection with the Mosaic System.

Second Modification of the general theory, held by a few Rabbins, who maintained that there was a literal tabernacle in the heavens and copied by Moses.

Third Modification.—That the Tabernacle represented the invisible heavens. 1. This is based on the fact that the Scriptures use the same terms in reference to the Tabernacle as of Heaven; e. g., "God dwelleth in both." 2. That Solomon, in his prayer,(I Kings, 8:30) asks that God would hear in heaven, &c., when they prayed toward the temple. 3. That this view has the authority of the N. T. Heb. 9:24; 9:11; 8:2; 6:20.

Against this we say: The apostle does establish a relationship between the Tabernacle and Heaven, but not that of a symbol but of a *type*. What was done by the priest in the Tabernacle was typical of what Christ does in Heaven.

As to the other arguments: God did dwell in the Tabernacle and in Heaven: but the Tabernacle was not the symbol of Heaven. He manifested himself in both, but in different ways. One was the abode of his condescension as the God of Israel, the other the abode of his glory as the God of *the Universe*.

[illegible] – Tabernacle [illegible]

[illegible]

[illegible]

The *true* meaning is shown by the different expressions used in reference to it. It is called the *tent* or *tabernacle* and *house of God*; the *palace* or *temple*, (1 Sam. 1 : 9) the *dwelling place of God*. *1* These names suggest the idea of earthly residence. God is not a God afar off, but near at hand. *2* The design was expressly declared by God himself (Ex. 25 : 8) as the place where he would dwell. God was there, and there spoke and manifested his presence. The people went up there to meet him and address him.

3 The character of the symbol itself: The house was designed for God, and placed in the centre of his camp. The several families of the Levites encamped near it, and three tribes on each side. It was set by the points of the compass, fronting the East, showing it to be set for the whole earth. His kingdom was to control all the earth; to correct the idea that the Jews were the exclusive favorites of heaven. *4* This general idea of God dwelling on the earth is further specified (Ex. 27 ; 21)=the Tabernacle of the congregation, which reads in Hebrew,=the Tent of meeting—a *meeting place* for two parties—Ex. 29 : 42–43. "Where I will meet you."—Ex. 25 : 22. The *purpose* of the meeting was—the Tabernacle of Testimony or Witness. See Num. 9 : 15 ; 18 : 2. God gave to Moses tables of testimony—Ex. 31 : 18 ; 25 : 16 ; Deut. 31 : 26. God's commandments are called testimony, because they testify God's will to men. This is the *Tabernacle* of testimony because it is the place where his will is made known. *5* The purpose for which God meets his people is shown in the name *Sanctuary* and also in the special names Holy Place and Holy of Holies. Called Sanctuary not because set apart for sacred duties ; still less in the sense of "asylum," which is a heathen idea.—These ideas are subordinate. But it did signify *inward moral purity*, the place where holiness is required and imparted. Lev. 21 : 23. The full idea then is—The place where God dwells with his people in order to testify his will and thus to sanctify them.

Examination of its structure and meaning of its parts.
1. The Tabernacle proper, ναός.
2. The Court, ἱερόν.

The Tabernacle was in the strict sense the House of God. The Court was not strictly so. Beyond the outer veil, the people could not pass, only the representatives of the people, the priests, could do so. The Tabernacle proper was divided by another veil—not by solid wall, indicating a permanent division. The veil formed an impassable barrier for the time to all but the High Priest. It was rent and access open to all at the crucifixion. The veil divided the Tabernacle into two unequal departments. 1. The Holy Place into which the Priests could all come. 2. Holy of Holies into which the High Priest could go, and he only on the great day of atonement.

The three stages of approach.
1. The Court opened to the people.
2. The Holy Place opened to the priests.
3. The Holy of Holies opened to the High Priest once a year.

These *representatives* secured access and showed that free entrance was only temporarily withheld. The gifts of the people could be taken in by the priests. The symbols of the people were in the Holy Place. These symbols showed that in time they might enter there.

The articles in the Holy of Holies signified God's relation to his people. Those in the Holy Place signified the relation of the people to God.

LECTURE II.

Description of the Ark.

It was a wooden chest, overlaid with gold, containing the two tables of the Law. The cover was a solid slab of gold on which the two cherubim beaten from the same slab.

Two Explanations.

First.—Based on the term "Ark of the testimony." Deut. 31 : 26. The book of the Law is here called a witness. Now it is said that this "book of the Law" is just an expansion of, or commentary upon the tables of the Law as delivered upon Mount Sinai. The book was put in the side of the ark and this reveals the purpose why the *tables* were put *in* the Ark. The "Tables of testimony" were so called because they are the testimony against the sins of the people. They say that the golden Mercy-seat covers up this testimony of the sins of the people: and that the Hebrew word signifies this. This is *defective.*

(a) When God pardons the sins of the people, he covers their guilt or sin but not the *Law*. The Law is not silenced but satisfied. Paul teaches that believers are free from the Law, but this is a New Testament declaration.

(b) The analogy of the book of the Law being put in the side of the Ark is against the case which it was drawn to adduce. The Books should have been put where the tables were, on this hypothesis.

(c) The name mercy-seat (KAPPORETH) does not mean cover or lid, as given by Gesenius. There is a Daghesh forte in the Pe, showing that the *Piel* is meant, signifying to propitiate or forgive sin. It was the place where the High Priest made expiation.

SECOND EXPLANATION.—The true view is this: The tables of the Law were God's covenant with Israel and therefore their most sacred treasure, kept in the Ark as a place of safety. The Golden Mercy-seat represents the Throne of God. God's mercy is based on his immutable Law. It was golden, to show the perfection and beauty of that mercy. Above the Mercy-seat, between the Cherubim, was the *Shekinah*, God's manifested glory. The cloud betokened his presence. From hence he spoke with Moses, Ex. 25: 22. Hence God is said to dwell between the Cherubim. He occupied this throne not for wrath or vengeance, but for mercy. It was the Mercy-seat to represent the presentation and acceptance of the blood of sacrifice. The *Cherubim* were composite figures, (Ex. 25: 20) having the face of a man and wings. Ez. 1: 5; 10: 20. The Cherubim are described, but not exactly the same as in Exodus—Man, Lion, Ox, Eagle. Shows the concentration in one of all the highest and noblest qualities in creation. The quintessence of creation. adoring and surrounding the throne of God. Such compound figures were familiar to the people of Assyria and Egypt, where Moses and Ezekiel lived. The Sphinx of Egypt consisted of the body of a lion and head of a man. The *Eagle* was the king of birds; the *Lion*, the king of beasts; the *Ox*, the chief of domestic animals; the *Man*, the highest of intelligent creation. The combination of these brings together the most noble of the animate creation. It is the entire animate creation condensed; the ideal embodiment of creation, and sets forth the noblest beings God has made. These were not actual representations, for the descriptions vary in different parts of Scripture. In Isaiah 6th, six wings are mentioned; Ez. 1:6, four faces and four wings; Ez. 41:18, every cherub had two faces; Rev. 4:7-8—six wings. Each beast represented one of the elements which constituted the Cherubim. These variations in form, while the general character remains the same, show that they are symbols and not exact images.

This appears first from other parts of Scripture. (1) Gen. 3:24, where first mentioned. (2) They are commonly represented as being in the immediate presence of God—Isaiah 6; Ezekiel 1; Ezekiel 10; Rev. 4:6; Psalms 18:10. (3) In the Mosaic Ritual they are at the ends of the Mercy-seat, and therefore near the Throne of God. The curtains were wrought with Cherubim. Ex. 26:1. So also the Veil—Ex 26:31. The High Priest could enter the Holy of Holies once a year, but the Cherubim remained there continually. So of the priests in the Holy Place and the Cherubim there. (4) The language of Peter, (1 Peter 1:12) contains an allusion supposed to refer to the posture of the Cherubim, with their faces toward the Ark. Therefore the Cherubim represented the Angels, the highest order of created beings. The pure gold represented their purity and extreme value. In Rev. 5:8-14, the beasts are represented as leading the praises of the universe. They were one piece with the Mercy-seat, therefore they are a part of God's throne, the ground of his dominion. They were two in number, in order to show, perhaps, that they were not a representation of God himself. The *Holy of Holies* was a perfect cube. The New Jerusalem mentioned in

39

Revelation, was also a perfect cube, which indicated perfection. The Holy of Holies had no artificial light. The Shekinah was the only light. The New Jerusalem needed no light, for God was the light.

Was the Shekinah *permanent?*—Ex. 40 : 35. (1) Some say that the brilliancy was confined to the times when it is mentioned. (2) Tradition says that it was continued down to the time of the Babylonish captivity, and this was one reason why the latter temple was inferior to the first. Lev. 16 : 2, implies that the Shekinah was there. Others think that the cloud meant the cloud of incense.

LECTURE III.

The *Holy Place* contained (1) the *Altar of Incense*, (2) the *Table of Shew Bread*, and (3) the *Candlestick*.

There are two directly opposite interpretations to these symbols.

I. That of *Baehr.* As these were in God's house, he supposes that they represented something belonging to or proceeding from God himself. The table was merely to receive the bread. The Shew Bread,(LEHEM HAPPANIM) or the bread of the face, of the Divine face, according to Baehr. The Bread of God which he provides for his people; twelve loaves,(Lev. 24 : 5) one for each tribe. It was removed every Sabbath, and what was taken away was eaten by the priests as the representatives of the people. Baehr says it represented the Bread of Life, " of which if a man eat, he shall live forever."

The *Candlestick* was for the sake of the light which it was to shed. Baehr says it is the light which God dispenses to his people. The seven branches denoted the perfection of the light—Rev. 4 : 5; Psalms 12 : 6. According to Baehr, it was the centre and seat of spiritual light and life. These two articles one on the north and the other on the south side, stand in relation to the third article placed between them directly in front of the ark, and separated from it only by a veil, i. e. the *Altar of Incense.* Baehr assumes that the incense means the diffusion of the *Name* of God, i. e. God as he is revealed, or his Spirit, himself veiled from sight but made known by the Spirit. The *light* and *life*-giving Spirit. Hence the meaning of the Shew Bread and Candlestick. Hence the Holy Place is the place where the Spirit is diffused as the source of spiritual *life and light*. This opinion is erroneous and at variance with Scripture. These articles represented what belonged to God, but not necessarily what proceeded from God. The furniture of the Holy Place represented what the people are to do in reference to God. The *Incense* was the symbol of *worship* and *prayer*.—Psalms 141 : 2; Rev. 5 : 8; 8 : 3–4; Luke 1 : 10; Num. 16 : 46. It represented the intercession of the High Priest.—Lev. 1 : 16 ; 7 : 9. To burn incense was to offer worship. It is often mentioned also in heathen worship. There is no symbol about which there is less difference of opinion.

The *Candlestick* is explained in Scripture—Rev. 1 : 12–20; Zech. 4. It was a symbol of the church or people of God. "Ye are the light of the world. Let your light so shine," &c. The lamps were fed with oil, which is a symbol of the Holy Spirit. It was used in anointing Priests and Kings to signify the gift of needed blessings. Referred to in 1 John 2 : 27. The oil in lamps represented the Holy Spirit given to the church as the source of their knowledge, holiness and joy.

The *Table of Shew Bread*, represented what the people of God are expected to do. Service to be rendered;—Lev. 24 : 8, 9. The Bread was not from God but to him from the people. 12 loaves=1 for each tribe. So each tribe had a share in the offering. Bread is the fruit of labor and toil, and represented so much labor done for God. It also represented their means of subsistence. It denoted that their lives and property were consecrated to God. It denoted the devotion of their activity to God's service. Symbol of good works. Hence incense was placed upon it, (Lev. 24 : 7) to denote the union of prayer and good works. The Bread was renewed every Sabbath, showing that good works are to be perpetual. None could eat it but the priests. This shows that they who work for God are fed from his table. David ate of it when in need, hence we see that the outward ceremony gave way to a case of necessity.

Have these articles of furniture any significance in themselves?

1. Some say not:—that they are only instrumental and have no inherent meaning, hence are not symbolic. This theory is not true for we know that the Candlestick was a symbol of the church.

2. Some say that the Altar and Table were symbols *per se*, as the Candlestick and the Altar represented the Church as the offerer of prayer, and the Table represented the Church as the bearer of good works. This is not conclusive for:

(a.) Although the Candlestick is a symbol, there is no such declaration as to the Table and the Altar.

(b) The Altar cannot be symbolical of the church, because it must always have the same meaning and this would not apply to the Altar of Burnt Offering in the Court. It would not explain the *horns* of the altar and the *atonement*.

(c) There was nothing in the construction of the Table or Altar to fit them for such symbolism, but in the *Candlestick* there was.

(d) There was a radical difference in their character. The *Candlestick* was an *agent* in producing light; the Altar and the Table were not agents in producing incense and bread and therefore cannot represent the church as the offerer and performer. They only receive what is prepared elsewhere. They were but vessels. The Bread on the table becomes the offering, and the incense on the altar. The table is thus a modified altar. Simply the place to which the offering is brought. The candlestick is not merely a place on which oil is poured but where light is *produced*. It is an instrument which, by the infusion of oil and fire, gives light. As to its *form* and *material*. The *Candlestick* was made of gold to indicate its purity—branching and with buds to indicate that the church is spreading, living, thriving and fruitful. The symbols of the Holy Place therefore represent the offerings of God's people, prayer and good works.

THE FURNITURE OF THE COURT:

The Brazen *Altar* and *Laver*.

1. Altar. This was for sacrifice and was called brazen from its hollow frame of boards overlaid with brass or

rather bronze. Ex. 22: 1-8. The Altar itself was made of earth and stones. Ex. 20 : 24, 25. This shows that the altar was not a human structure in its conception, but an ascent toward heaven, signifying drawing near to God. Thus Noah sacrificed on Mt. Ararat; Abraham on Mt. Moriah; Moses and Aaron communed with God on top of Mt. Sinai. Ex. 24: 9. There was a tendency to worship God on the tops of mountains and high hills and in groves, whose silence denoted solemnity. Gen. 21: 3₴ Other nations had this idea. Mt. Olympus in Greece was the abode of their Gods. An altar represented a mountain in miniature, an ascent toward heaven, and God comes down to meet the offerer there. When the Greeks offered to the Gods of the lower world. they offered in trenches. The word altar in the Heb. MIZBEHA″=to lift up. Altar from *altus* high—Greek βῆμα from βαίνω. Ex. 20: 24. There was such a place to meet God in each division of the Tabernacle. In the Court, the Altar of Burnt Offering; in the Holy Place, the Altar of Incense; and the Mercy-seat in the Holy of Holies. The divine presence was to be met in each, and expiation and forgiveness given in each of these places. This rendered the Tabernacle the house of meeting and entitled it to the name of the House of God. (2.) The *Laver*,—Ex. 30: 18. It is less minutely described than any other article in the Tabernacle. It was for Aaron and his sons to wash in, when they went into the Tabernacle or approached the Altar,—Ex. 30: 19-21. This symbolized the need of purity. The hands doing God's will and the feet treading on sacred ground. Moses at the burning bush, and Joshua in the presence of the captain of the Lord's host, were directed to loose their shoes from off their feet. The *Laver*, (Ex. 38: 8) was made of the looking-glasses or metallic mirrors of the women. These mirrors were converted into instruments of cleansing and this was an instance of consecrating what was secular to sacred ends.

LECTURE IV.

Sacrifices. There are two classes of sacred actions, offerings and purifications. Offerings were the most sacred and could be performed only at the Sanctuary.

Purification could be performed anywhere. The word offering=KARBAN= δῶρον =gift. This word, used also in Mark 7:11, denotes anything brought near to God, and hence includes what was brought to adorn the Sanctuary and to maintain the Priests.
1. Gifts for the House of God.
2. "   "   Ministers of God.
3. "   "   God himself=offerings.
Those designed for the Altar, are: (a.) Animal or bloody. (b.) Vegetable or bloodless. The first consisted of oxen, sheep and goats and in cases of extreme poverty, doves and pigeons. The second consisted of grain and flour, oil and wine, bread or cakes. Salt and incense were added as an accompaniment but were not a part of the offering. Honey and leaven were expressly prohibited.

Why were these particular objects offered? The answer depends on the ideas held as to what the sacrifice represented.

I. *Materialistic View.* That it was intended as food for the deity. These were given him because they were the usual articles of food, which he needed as well as light and shelter. Answer—1. This is utterly inconsistent with the character of God. It is opposed to the *Spirituality* of God, which was constantly taught. Ps. 50:12-13. 2. The principal and most essential element of the sacrifice was blood, and this was expressly prohibited as food.

II. *Pecuniary View.* That the sacrifice was a penalty or fine exacted as a condition of pardon; and that the material offered represented their wealth and property. Answer—1. The prominence given to blood is not explained by this. 2. The limitation in the objects offered is not explained. Why would not camels, asses, costly garments and furniture answer equally well?

III. *Exclusively Typical View.* That the sole design was to prefigure Christ and his work, and the materials selected were to set forth his personal qualities of a Redeemer, or his official character, or the nature of his work. Answer—This is defective for: (1.) It is a mistake to suppose that this is the *sole* object. The design of types is to set forth truths and not to delineate objects.

(2.) This leads to far-fetched explanations and analogies. If a lamb was sacrificed to represent Christ, why not a Lion, since he was called the Lion of the tribe of Judah? Why were bulls and goats sacrificed, since they are represented in the Scriptures as enemies, (Ps. 22 : 12 and Matt. 25 : 3) and why not the roe and hart, Canticles 2 : 17 ?

What particular qualities were each designed to represent ? Why were different animals offered, and why of different age and sex ? Why sacrificed at different times ? Why grain, and why so prepared ? Some say that the fine flour represented Christ's sufferings from the fact of its being ground ; and cakes, because they were prepared by fire. (3.) These allusions would have been utterly unintelligible to the Jews, and thus the types would have failed of their object.

IV. *Spiritualistic View.* That the sacrifice represented the inward spiritual transaction of the offerer. The animal represented the offerer. The death of the animal represented his death for sin. The presentation of blood represented the consecration of his life to God, hence those objects are proper to be offered which best serve as symbols of the offerer.

Answer—(1.) A sacrifice would then signify an inward change of heart but no atonement for sin. Lev. I : 4. (2.) There is no foundation in Scripture for the assumption that the sacrifice represented the offerer himself. It symbolized not a sinner but a sinless being. The heathen offerings vary according to the divinity and not according to the offerer. The animal was not chosen as a representative of man, but as one acceptable to the divinity. (3.) The thing to be represented is forgiveness and purification. This, the sacrifice of the animal could not teach. There is nothing to suggest a return to spiritual life. The animal remains dead, unlike the case of the purification of the leper. Lev. 14 : 49–53.

V. The *True View.* That the offerings were to set forth (a) Expiation for sin, and (b) Consecration to God;= a vicarious atonement and an *oblation* to God. The animal sacrifices showed both, the vegetable only the latter. The victim is not a symbol of the offerer, but a substitute. The substitute is slain ; showing that the forfeited life has been taken. The arguments in favor of this :

3

1. This is the old *traditional view*.
2. This will explain all forms of the service.
3. This is in accordance with scripture.
4. This is conformable to the design of Christ's death.
5. This presents the most satisfactory explanation for the limitation of animals in the sacrifice. An oblation
    (1.) Must be his own possession.
    (2.) The product of his toil. This excludes spontaneous productions, and fruits and wild animals.
    (3.) It should be his food by which his life is sustained, as a pledge of his life being consecrated to God. This excludes what may be raised for show, &c.
    A *Substitute* must be (1.) an animal having a life to give. Lev. 5: 11 is the only exception, and it proves the rule. (2.) This life must be a sinless life, not only negatively but positively, at least in a symbolic and ceremonial sense. This last consideration excludes human sacrifice. (3.) Yet a substitute should possess a community of nature with the offerer, hence the use of domestic animals as being most closely allied to man.

LECTURE V.

Meaning of the acts included in the Animal Sacrifice, Lev. 1: 1–9. After the presentation of the victim at the Tabernacle the sacrificial service included: 1. Laying on of hands. 2. Killing the victim. 3. Sprinkling the blood. 4. Burning the animal either whole or in part. Besides these there were, 5. Pecuniary compensation in the trespass offering, and 6. A sacrificial feast in the peace offering. The first four were common to all sacrifices.

I. Laying on of hands, Lev. 1: 4. The offerer put his hand on the head of the animal. The imposition of hands is always employed in Scripture to denote the impartation of something by a person authorized or qualified to do so.

(1) *Giving Blessing.* Gen. 48: 13, 14; Matt. 19: 12–15.

(2) *Giving Holy Ghost.* Acts 8: 17–18; 19: 6.

(3) *Conferring Office.* Deut. 34:9; Num. 8:~~10~~, /0 Acts 6:6; I. Tim. 4:14.
(4) *Impartation of Miraculous Virtue.* Matth. 9:18; Mark. 6:5.
(5) *Witnesses laid hands on a blasphemer's head.* Lev. 24:14.

This ceremony always denotes the impartation of something, and refutes all views in which this element is not found.

First View. Philo says that it is an exhibition of the hands of the offerer, and denotes his innocence. This is not true, for a different ceremony would have been more appropriate, such as the washing of hands. E. g. Pilate.

Second View. That it designated the animal as the property of the offerer, corresponding to the Roman ceremony of manumission of slaves, and his consecration of it to God. But both these ideas were shown sufficiently by the act of bringing the animal to the Sanctuary.

Third View. That it was a solemn *consecration* of the victim, but if so, the priest, and not the offerer, would have laid his hand upon it.

Fourth and true View. It can only mean that the *guilt* of the offerer is transferred to the victim—not his moral character, but his liability to punishment. This appears:

(1.) From express explanation of this ceremony in Lev. 16:21. (2.) It may be inferred from the position which the laying on of hands holds in the sacrificial service. It occurs in all animal sacrifices, except that of doves, and never in the vegetable offerings. This shows that it must be related to something peculiar to the animal sacrifice, i. e., the atonement. This act is done by the offerer, and not by the priest, and therefore indicates something connected with himself. It also follows the presentation of the victim and immediately precedes the slaughter. The effect of imposition of hands is to qualify the victim to make atonement for the sin of the offerer. Lev. 1:4. (3.) This is the ancient, traditional, and commonly received explanation.

Some recent interpreters have made a distinction in the signification of this ceremony in the different

kinds of sacrifices. Holding that in the *sin-offering*, it denoted a transfer of the guilt of the offerer, but in the *burnt-offering* it signified the desire of the offerer to be consecrated to God. In the *peace-offering* it denoted gratitude and thankfulness to God. *Reply.* (a.) Although the ultimate aim is different in each, the immediate end is the same in all, i. e., atonement for sin. (b.) The transfer of legal relations is easily comprehended, but we cannot conceive of a transfer of the emotions of the offerer. (c.) Lev. 1 : 4, expressly says that the acceptance of the atonement depends on the laying on of hands in the burnt-offering. The hands were laid on the head not for convenience sake, but because the penalty was a capital one.

II. Slaying of the Sacrifice. The infliction of the penalty. It showed the doctrine of substitution which is taught in Isaiah 53. *Various views.*

1. Some say that slaying here means only renunciation of the victim and surrender of it to God on the part of the offerer. The death rendering it useless to the offerer. Complete consecration to God. This falls with the error on which it is based, which is not analogous to the Roman custom of manumission.

2. *Spiritualistic View.*—That it represented the dying of a sinful nature and the giving up of a worldly life, and obtaining communion with God by presentation at his altar.

Answer—(1.) The victim was not a symbol of the offerer, but a sinless substitute. (2.) The life of the animal cannot represent a sinful life. The imputation of sin transfers the liability to punishment, and not the moral character. Christ was our substitute, but did not possess our sinful nature. (3.) The death of one to whom sin is imputed cannot be the medium of bringing the offerer near to God, except as being a substitute for him. (4.) This makes inward holiness the ground of pardon, and sanctification to precede justification. The death of the animal here means that the offerer thus dies unto sin, whereas his sin must be atoned for as a preliminary to his being brought into communion with God.

3. This view regards the *slaying* as merely an indispensable means of securing the blood and flesh, and has no signification in or of itself.

Answer—(1.) The slaying of the victim was an integral part of the ritual, prescribed to be done at the Tabernacle in the presence of the priests, &c. (2.) This is tantamount to a confession that it is the penalty of the law endured in the offerer's stead.

4. *Penal View.*—It has been objected to this true penal view, (1) that the victim was slain by the offerer and not by the priest.

Answer—(a.) The sinner is his own destroyer. (b.) The sinner is his own accuser and confessor. (c.) It is typically significant of Christ. Doves *were* slain by the priests because of the scarcity of blood.

Objection (2.)—This makes the slaying of more consequence than the sprinkling. Answer—(a.) In a judicial view, it is still the sprinkling which actually effects the expiation. (b.) The slaying is an equally essential part of the ritual.

III. *Sprinkling of the Blood.—Different Views.*—1. That it was the *complement* to the act of slaying. This is not so, for (a.) The blood was not wasted but carefully gathered, and (b.) It was brought to a specified place and used in a prescribed way.

2. *Spiritualistic View.*—That the bringing of the blood, which is the life, to the altar, represented that the life of the offerer shall be made holy and sanctified. Answer—(a.) According to Lev. 1: 4; 7: 11, the blood makes the atonement and is not itself atoned for. (b.) It is distinguished from the offerer as making the atonement for him, not as a symbol but a *substitute*.

3. The blood was sprinkled upon the sacred vessels, because they were regarded as defiled by the sins of the people, and the blood covered this defilement. This is argued from Lev. 16: 15-19. Answer—(a.) It would be more natural to sprinkle the offerer himself, who was the sinner. (b.) A separate service was used for the atonement of the Sanctuary once a year, but not in every sacrifice.

4. *True View.*—It is an exhibition at the altar of the blood which has been shed for the offerer, and represents expiation and that death has been suffered. The blood was sprinkled (1) on the Brazen Altar; (2) at the Golden Altar of Incense; (3) at the Mercy seat—at places where God especially met with his people. The fact of his requiring it to be placed there, denoted his acceptance of it.

IV. *Burning* of the Victim at the Altar. With the sprinkling, the atonement was completed. Now comes the oblation, which was accomplished by burning the victim. This was common to the animal and vegetable offering. Some regarded the fire as the wrath of God, showing that temporal death did not exhaust the penalty of the law, but that the vengeance of eternal fire should follow. Answer—(a.) Fire may be regarded as a purifier as well as a destroyer. It leaves the earthly portion here and carries the rest heavenward. (b.) The whole penalty of the law is represented by the death of the victim. (c.) This burning follows the sprinkling, by which expiation has been already effected. (d.) The victim is said to be a sweet savor unto the Lord.—Lev. 1 : 9. (e.) The bloodless offering was also burned on the altar. There was no sin represented in these offerings, hence the symbol must mean the same in both cases. The fire carries the sacrifice to God relieved from all earthly dross. It is an oblation of food made to him—Lev. 21 : 6-8. It is a tribute returned to God for most necessary gifts—not to absolve from further consecration, but pledges property, labor and life, all to God. Rom. 12 : 1 ; Psalms 40 : 6-8. The animal was skinned, for the skin was not used for food, and the flesh washed, so that the offering might be clean—free from defilement.

LECTURE VI.

Different Kinds of Sacrifice.

They were <u>not</u> first instituted by Moses. They existed from the earliest Bible History. Moses modified, regulated and enlarged them. What had been left to the pleasure of the offerer, was now explicitly determined by Divine statute. Rigor, precision and complexity succeed simplicity, &c. This was progress. The elements were separated and made distinct to the mind of the offerer with an ultimate reference to Christ. The *Burnt-offering* was the principal form in the *Patriarchal System*. Besides this was the "*Sacrifice*." Gen. 46: 1. In Ex. 10:25, this is distinguished from the burnt-offering. In Gen. 31: 54, a sacrificial feast formed part of the service. This must have corresponded to the Peace-offering. *Vegetable-offering*, Gen. 4: 3; *Drink-offering*, Gen. 35: 14.—That these were not distinct offerings in former times appears from Gen. 8: 20, where Noah offers a *Burnt-offering*. The Mosaic ritual would have required a *Peace*-offering. See also Job 1: 5; 42: 8. *Burnt*-offerings instead of *Sin*-offerings.

There were two *ideas* in the Sacrifices: 1. *Atonement*—Expiation by sprinkling of blood. 2. *Oblation*—Consecration by burning on the altar. The Sin-offering emphasizes Atonement. The Burnt-offering emphasizes Oblation.

There were two other offerings: 3. *Trespass*-offering, with the idea of satisfaction by pecuniary compensation. 4. *Peace*-offering, with the idea of restored communion with God by means of a sacrificial feast. When different kinds of sacrifices are to be offered together they are invariably named *in order*, and Sin-offering always precedes Burnt-offering, and both of these before the *Peace*-offering. Ex. 29: 14, 18, 25; Judges 20: 26; Ez. 45: 17. The Sin and Trespass-offerings were designed to restore the Theocratic relations with God. The Burnt and Peace-offerings, to express and maintain these relations.

I. DISTINCTION BETWEEN THE SIN AND TRESPASS-OFFERINGS. *Various Opinions.*—1. That there was no real difference. The offerer could do as he chose. 2. That the Sin-offering was for sins of ignorance, and the Trespass-offering for *venial* sins. 3. That the Sin-offering was for sins of omission, and the Trespass-offering for sins of commission. 4. That the Sin-offerings were for sins voluntarily confessed, and the Trespass-offerings for sins

proven by testimony. 5. That the Sin-offering was for lighter sins, and the Trespass-offering for more serious offences.

The True View.—That the Sin-offering was for simple transgression of the Law, and the Trespass-offering for trespass or injury against God or fellow-men, for which amends must be made together with one-fifth in addition. The Trespass-offering was also required in cleansing a leper, because he must make amends for his lack of service to God during his defilement. Also required of a Nazarite who had a special vow, and had contracted ceremonial uncleanness in the meantime. The *ritual* of these two offerings was determined by their character and design. The animal varied according to the theocratic standing of the offerer, in the Sin-offering. For the sins of the entire people, or of the High Priest as the representative of the people, a young bullock was required. For an ordinary ruler, a *he*-goat. For one of the common people, a *she*-goat or sheep. For the poor, two doves or pigeons. For extreme poverty, one-tenth of an ephah of flour. The enormity of the sin was aggravated by the standing of the sinner. This *gradation* is peculiar to the *Sin*-offering. In the *Trespass*-offering, a *ram* was required in every case, because the damage was the same, irrespective of the wealth of the offerer. The *Sin*-offering was for the whole people, and was offered at the annual *feasts*, to atone for the sins of the whole people in the *interval*.

No Trespass-offering was required, because the nature of this required the particular sin to be made known. Only a *single* animal was offered in the Sin and Trespass-offering. There was an indefinite number in the Burnt and Peace-offerings. Because in the Sin and Trespass-offerings the expiation for sin was the pure act of God's grace, and not to be purchased by the number of the offerings. In the Burnt and Peace-offerings, which represented the inward devotion of the heart, and therefore could be intensified, an indefinite number of victims might be offered. At the dedication of the *temple*, tens and hundreds of thousands were offered. The great idea of the Trespass-offering is satisfaction for sin, reparation for damage by pecuniary compensation. In the

Sin-offering, the prominence is given to the sprinkling of blood, and the great idea is expiation for sin. The blood was brought to the altar in every sacrifice; but in the others it was sprinkled round about the altar, while in the Sin-offering a greater formality was required.

(1.) *In the case of the High-Priest.* The blood was taken by the Priest on his finger, and smeared on the horns of the altar; these were the vertices or culminating points, the idea being that the virtue in it rose to its maximum. The rest of the blood was poured at the base of the altar. See Lev. 4 : 3–12.

(2.) *In the case of the sin of the whole people.* The blood was carried into the Holy Place and sprinkled seven times in front of the rail, and was also taken on the finger of the Priest and put on the horns of the Golden Altar of Incense, while he poured the rest of the blood at the base of the Altar in the court. Lev. 13 : 21. On the great Day of Atonement, the High Priest took the blood of the *sin-offering* and sprinkled it upon the mercy-seat in the Holy of Holies.

In the case of the *Sin and Trespass-offering*, the fat only was to burned on the altar; the flesh was given to the Priests to be eaten in the court, in case the sacrifice was for a layman; but if for the priest or for the whole people, it was to be burned in a clean place without the camp. Lev. 6 : 25.

Different Explanations of this rule.

These offerings were made unholy by the sin imputed to them; therefore the flesh could not be burned with acceptance on God's altar, but must be consumed in some other way, either outside the camp or be eaten by the priests. This symbolized the annihilation of the sin which had been imputed to it. If eaten, it was supposed to be absorbed in the holiness of the priests. If the priest was the sinner, or the people, then the holiness required to consume the sin was lacking. Hence the flesh must be burned. In support of this, those who hold it quote Lev. 10 : 17. They inferred that the eating of the Sin-offering by Aaron and his sons was equal to consuming the sin of the people. This is not necessarily the meaning of the passage. That this view is not correct appears from Lev. 16 : 25 and 10 : 17. The flesh is there called "most holy," also Lev. 6: 26-29. It was eaten only in the Holy Place, and anything it touched was made holy by it. It must be washed in the Holy Place, and a brazen pot in which it was sodden must be rinsed and scoured, and an earthen vessel was to be broken. The fat was burned on the Altar. This would not have been so, if there were any defilement in the animal; nor would the priest be allowed to eat defilement. The sin had already been atoned for, by the sprinkling of the blood before the flesh was to be eaten. The burning of it outside the camp, in a clean place whither the ashes had been carried, was analogous to the burning of what was left from the Passover and Peace-offering, and was to preserve it from decay and corruption. The priests could not eat the sacrifice offered for themselves, because they could not profit by their own sins. They were God's servants, and therefore were to be fed from his table.

II. BURNT-OFFERING.—Emphasized oblation and consecration. Its characteristic was the burning of the whole eatable portion of the animal. It could be offered at any time, and was the most frequent of the offerings. The other offerings were for special occasions. There was a regular public Burnt-offering for every day, consisting of a lamb every morning and evening. The fire was never allowed to go out. On the Sabbath, the daily Burnt-offering was doubled. On the first of the month there was a larger offering; and at the annual feast, larger still. It was the only kind of offering that could be offered alone. No act of worship was acceptable without the consecration which the burnt-offering represented. Any kind of *clean* animals might be offered. It must be without blemish and a *male*, except in the case of *Dores*, where there was but little difference in the size of the two sexes, (and yet the *masculine* suffix is used in the case of *Dores*.) In the Sin-offering, where gradation was required, this was made in part by distinction of gender. Males were considered higher than females. The female was not allowed in the Burnt-offering at all. Some say that the male represented greater strenuousness, &c., on the part of the offerer, to God's service. But difference in size is the most plausible explanation.

LECTURE VII.

III. THE PEACE-OFFERING—To express and ratify peace with God. Its characteristic feature was a *feast*, which signified peace and communion with God. When this Sacrifice is mentioned in a series, it is the highest and last. Three kinds are recognized.
 1. *Thanksgiving* in acknowledgement of some benefit from God, or for God's mercy in general.
 2. *Vows* in fulfillment of pledges previously given.
 3. *Free-will* offering of the inward, spontaneous impulse.

Peace-offerings were presented for benefits desired, as well as for benefits received. Judges 20: 26; 21: 4; 1 Sam. 13: 9; 2 Sam. 24: 25.

Any sacrificial animal, male or female might be presented, according to the wish of the offerer. It could be male or female. Doves and pigeons are not mentioned, because this sacrifice was not urgent, and so the very poor did not need to offer at all. Moreover, doves and pigeons would have been unsuitable for the sacrificial feast which followed. The animal must be without blemish. Only in the free-will offering one " superfluous or lacking in its parts " might be presented. It was a spontaneous gift, so an animal of less value would be accepted.

The disposition of the *flesh* was peculiar to this kind of sacrifice. The fat was burned on the altar. The *breast* and *right (shoulder* or*) ham* were waved or heaved and given to the priests; the ham to the friends who ministered in this particular sacrifice, and the breast to the priests in general.

There was no particular meaning in them, as that the breast=" affection," and the shoulder="work." These are called technically the *wave breast* and *heave shoulder*, because of the consecration by waving and heaving. There is a tradition about this ceremony. The waving was by some supposed to be a horizontal motion toward each of the four points of the compass. Others think that it was waved forward, toward the sanctuary, and then backward again. This, they say, showed it to be

given to God and then God gave it to the priests. The *heaving* was the raising of it up to heaven and lowering it again.

The rest of the flesh was given to the offerer, who, with his family and friends and some needy Levites, ate it. This symbolized communion with God and his people.

1. *The Spiritualistic View.* That the animal represented the offerer himself. Part was given to God on the altar, and part given to the priests, (i. e., God's people,) and thus the offerer was brought into union and fellowship with God and his people. The objections to this view are:

(1) The offence eats a symbol of himself. He was not excluded from the sacrificial feast.

(2) The priests and the friends form two separate companies, but according to this they should be one.

2. *The True View.* That this is a feast in which God is the host, and the offerer and friends are guests. This appears: (1.) The flesh was the flesh of a sacrifice which belonged wholly to the Lord. (2.) Not only that which was burned, but that which was eaten, is called the "bread of God." Lev. 7: 20–21; 21: 22. (3.) It was to be eaten before the Lord in his court. (4.) From N. T., 1 Cor. 10: 18–21, we learn that the offerer is the guest of that deity of whose sacrifice he eats. (5.) Analogy of the Lord's supper, and of the parables of our Lord. (6.) This view is necessary to the significance of the emblems. This feast is a symbol of and a pledge of friendship, peace, and communion with God. It is upon the flesh of a sacrificial animal, and in an inward appreciation of the benefits of the sacrifice. The guests represented the whole body of God's people. It was impossible for them all to get together in one place and at one time, (except in such a case as the dedication of the temple,) and so a selection must be made. And the family and friends composed the company and represented the entire body of God's people. So, in the case of the Passover, each company *represented* the entire people of God. So also in the Lord's supper. What remained was to be burned and thus preserved from contamination and cor-

ruption. There was a distinction between the thank-offering and the vow or free-will-offering. The *thank-offering* was the holiest, and hence corruption was more strictly guarded against. No part of it was to be left until the next day. Lev. 7: 15.

The *Vow* and *free-will* offering could be left until the second day. Lev. 7: 16–21; 19: 6.

The *Bloodless* or *Vegetable* or Meat-offering, (Heb., MINHAH.) "Meat," in our English version,="food." The *meat*-offering was distinguished from the *drink*-offering, and yet it often included all vegetable offerings. The materials were the three products, grain, oil, and wine. Ps. 104: 15. Fruits of trees and garden herbs were excluded.

Baehr finds a correspondence between these materials and those of the animal-offerings, viz., bread=flesh, oil =fat, wine=blood. This he says is the reason why meal is sometimes allowed. Lev. 6: 11. This is imaginary, for oil was forbidden in the meal when offered as a sin-offering; and wine cannot represent blood, which was forbidden to be drunk. Grain could be offered (a) as *grain* or *grits*, (b) as *flour*, fine flour, (c) as *bread* or *cakes*. A handful of flour or a cake was burned on the altar as a memorial before God. (It signified the same as the flesh in the animal sacrifice. It was an oblation of food, and represented the consecration of labor and life to God.) The rest was given to the priests, who ate it in the court. Lev. 6: 16. Thus God's servants were to be fed at his table. If presented by the priest, none was eaten, (Lev. 6: 23) because they were not to profit by their own sins. *Oil* was not a separate constituent, but an adjunct, (1) because the oil was not used separately, but mingled; (2) the oil is co-ordinated with incense (Lev. 2: 15); (3) oil was not an actual article of food, but was used in preparing it. It is spoken of in connection with bread and wine. Hence, it represented not a separate gift, or that which yields the light of knowledge, but here as elsewhere, it represented the Holy Spirit, without whom the sacrifice would not be complete or acceptable.

SALT and INCENSE.—*Salt* was used, because it represented preservation, the opposite of decay. A covenant of salt=a lasting covenant. Meat which endures. *Incense* was an accompaniment. It was burned on the offering but not mixed with it. *All* the incense was burned. It represented *prayer*, which must hallow every oblation. *Honey* and *Leaven* were prohibited. Leaven leads to fermentation and corruption, hence it was a symbol of evil. 1 Cor. 5 : 6–8. Honey also turns to sourness and corruption.

The *drink offering* was a separate oblation, but was added to the meat-offering. It consisted of wine, not poured at the base of the altar, but *upon* the altar. The drink on the table. Ex. 30 : 9. We know this to be true also from the analogy of heathen offerings. The *vegetable*-offerings were never presented *alone*, but must follow a *burnt* or *peace*-offering. The only instances to the contrary are the sin-offering of meal in poverty, and in the offering of jealousy. Num. 5 : 15.

LECTURE VIII.

Purification of the Mosaic Law.

These form the second class of Sacred actions. They were designed to symbolize the removal of the defilement and pollution of sin, as the removal of guilt was represented by the sacrificial expiation. The distinction of clean and unclean was made by the Levitical Law. The design of these minute regulations was not to promote 1. *Cleanliness* and decency among the people; because (a) in that case, everything filthy would have been ceremonially unclean. This was not the case. The number of objects was limited. (b) The idea of personal purity and ceremonial cleanliness are *distinct*. (c) The Orientals are careful about the latter and negligent about the former. (d) The religious character of the purifications is not explained by this view.

2. The design was not *Sanitary*, i. e., to promote the health of the people. (a) This view entirely overlooks the religious character of the institutions. The Purifications belong to the same order with the Sacrifices, and pertain to

a like end; and it would be in contradiction to the Mosaic system to suppose that religion was only a cover to some secular end. (b) This view will not account for what these laws contain or omit. A person may come in contact with any disease except *leprosy* without becoming defiled, but could not come into the presence of a dead body.

3. Nor was there anything wrong or peculiarly sinful in those things which were called unclean.

(a) There was nothing morally wrong in eating one animal and not another. The unclean animals had no connection with the kingdom of evil. (b) Nor was there any sin involved in those conditions of the human body which were considered unclean. E. g., no sin was connected with the natural birth of children. Barrenness was even regarded as a curse in those times. So the corpse of a good man was as defiling as that of a bad man. (c) Defilement might arise from actions which were actual duties; e. g., the burial of a relative, and certain other services which the ritual prescribed, and which could not be neglected.

The Distinction in Animals had a two-fold purpose.

1. It carried a distinction of right and wrong, duty and transgression, into the ordinary matters of daily life.

2. These laws were practically a wall of separation between Israel and the Gentiles, with whom (Acts 10 : 28) they could not so much as eat. This distinction in animals had relation only, first, to *food*, and, secondly, to the *worship of God*. Clean animals only could be eaten or sacrificed. Other animals could be used for any other purpose. The criteria of distinction were drawn partly from the organs of motion, and partly from food. In *beasts*, both were regarded. Those were clean which had the parted hoof and chewed the cud. In *fish*, those which had fins and scales were clean. This referred only to the organs of motion. In *birds*, food was the characteristic. Birds of prey were unclean. The distinction between clean and unclean was not without foundation in the nature of things. The rules were simple and clear, and embraced the chief, if not all, of the animals used for food. One class represented the idea of pure and clean,

the other that of unclean. It has been *supposed* that it was designed to suggest that those who belonged to God's kingdom were distinguished by their *walk* and *food*. This may be stretching the matter too far. This distinction is only a reflection of man's state of defilement in the presence of God. When men come near to God, or He to them, they must be cleansed from impurity. Ex. 19: 10–14; Lev. 8: 6; Ex. 30: 20; Num. 8: 7. None but the pure could come near the holy God.

But besides these rare occasions, and the select few engaged in sacred functions, the idea of clean and unclean was to receive a symbolical representation which should carry it into the affairs of daily life. The defilement was not that arising from voluntary sin, but from the involuntary and hereditary taint of sin in all men. This was denoted by selecting the extremes of life—*birth* and *death*. Birth is the source of human corruption, and *death* the final result of it. Each of these had its own specific curse attached to it in the fall of our first parents. These are the two poles about which ceremonial defilement centred, creating two classes of impurity. First. Everything relating to *birth* was defiled; everything sexual, whether natural or diseased, though not necessarily involving sin. See Lev., Chapters 12 and 15. The series culminated in birth. The measure and gradation of defilement was indicated by three particulars:

(1.) The length of *time* during which the uncleanness continued.

(2) The extent to which this defilement could be communicated.

(3) The character of the ritual necessary to its removal. All this was very complicated.

We will consider them in order.

(1) The Duration was various. It might be till *evening* only; in grosser cases for a week, measured from the beginning of the uncleanness, or the cessation of its cause; or for 40 days or twice 40. Forty was a sacred number. The four sides of a square, (the symbol of regularity) multiplied by 10, (the symbol of completeness) =40. Israel was in the wilderness 40 years. The period of defilement at the birth of a male child was 40 days;

of a female, 80 days. These longer periods were subdivided into two parts,—the first period consisting of 7 or 14 days, and the second of 33 or 66 days. The grade of defilement was greater during the first 7 or 14 days.

(2) The liability of the defilement to be communicated varied. The lighter kind was not transmissible. The more serious affected all who came in contact with the one so defiled. The most serious kind defiled not only the clothes, bed, etc., but every thing that was touched or spit upon.

(3) The mode of effecting purification varied also. (a) By simple washing of the person and clothes in water; or (b) in addition, he must bring two doves or young pigeons to the Sanctuary, one for the burnt-offering and the other for the sin-offering: or (c) a lamb of the first year for the burnt-offering and a turtle-dove for the sin-offering.

The Second Source of Ceremonial Defilement was *Death*;—either contact with a dead body, or leprosy, which was a sort of living death. Num. 12: 12. The eating of a clean animal which died of itself or was torn by wild beasts, was a source of defilement. Ex. 22: 31; Lev. 11: 39; 17: 15. Also to touch the dead carcass of an unclean beast. Lev. 11: 24–28. A human corpse was still more defiling. This appears (a) from the duration of the uncleanness which was for 7 days; (b) in its communicability. Num. 19: 14; (c) in the ritual for cleansing. The washing with water was not enough here, not even pure running water, but ashes must be mingled with it, and these ashes must be prepared in a peculiar and significant way. The ashes were those of a sin-offering, prepared with peculiar rites for this special purpose. Hence this exhibits sin, not only as defilement to be washed away, and shows the necessity of a sacrificial atonement, but also shows that this atonement is an indispensable prerequisite to the cleansing. The customary sin-offering was a young bullock. Lev. 4: 14. But this sin-offering was a *red heifer*. In ordinary sin-offerings, the color was indifferent. The *red* was a symbol of life and vigor,—being the color of *blood*. " To prepare an antidote to death," refers to the means of purification from contact with a corpse. The heifer must be one upon which a yoke had never rested to impair its vigor. This heifer, unlike the ordinary sin-offering, was not to be taken to the door of the tabernacle and there slain; but it must be brought without the camp and slain there by the eldest son of the High Priest and the blood sprinkled 7 times toward the Sanctuary. It was then burned whole and the ashes gathered by a clean man and put in a clean place outside the camp, to be used in purifying. Those officiating in this service were all rendered unclean and were required to wash their clothing, etc. This exclusion from the sanctuary and all the defilement resulting from the ceremony brought the whole service into connection with the idea of defilement and pollution, and was performed in relation to it. Thus the ceremony was defiling, though a duty. So the lesson is taught:—we may contract defilement in holy services. While the heifer was burning, the priest cast into the flames *cedar wood, hyssop,* and *scarlet. Cedar* was incorruptible; hyssop was used in cleansing; and scarlet was the color of blood, suggesting life. These ashes, mingled with running water, were sprinkled upon the unclean person from a bunch of hyssop, on the third and seventh days, and after bathing and washing his clothes, he shall be clean at evening. Num. 19: 19. And the persons who officiated, and any who touched the water, were rendered unclean.

Leprosy was but a living death. Very minute specifications are given, (Num. 14,) by which the priests could detect it. Read Lev. 13 and 14 chapters, for the mode of purification. The rites of cleansing consisted of two parts. The first effected the restoration to *civil* rights; the second to the communion of the Sanctuary. In order to the first, two living birds were taken, one as a sacrifice for the offerer, the other as a symbol of himself. The former was killed over running water, and the living bird was then dipped in the mixture of blood and water and the leper sprinkled 7 times with it. The leper was then pronounced clean and the bird let loose. After washing, bathing and shaving, and a probation of 7 days, he was admitted to full civil rights. See Lev.

14: 8, 9. His restoration to the privileges of the Sanctuary was effected on the following day. A *Trespass, Sin, Burnt* and *Meat*-offering were to be made; a *trespass*-offering in compensation for lack of service. Blood and oil were taken. Lev. 14: 12-19. This signified the application of the benefits of the sacrifice to the organs of hearing, doing, and running to obey God's commands. Oil signified the Holy Spirit. The sin-offering (Lev. 14: 19) was added to the satisfaction of the trespass-offering, as an atonement for the sin which the leprosy represented. Restoration being thus effected, the burnt and meat-offerings signified consecration of self and life. Read Lev., chapters 13 and 14, and Num. 19; also, in Smith's Dictionary, the article on Purification.

LECTURE IX.

Sacred Persons—Were those who were admitted to Sacred Places and entrusted with the performance of Sacred Rites? Man had forfeited the right of access to God, and no act of service rendered by him was acceptable. None could approach God, save those whom He chose. Israel was God's peculiar people—a holy nation. They were God's people in a special sense, and had the privilege of access to Him in a special way. In the encampment in the wilderness, the Tabernacle was placed in the centre of the encampment. God thus dwelt in the midst of his people. They also had access to the court of his Tabernacle. Within the square formed by the encampment of the tribes around the Tabernacle, was another square in which dwelt the Sacerdotal Tribe of *Levi* and the *Priests*. The Levites were chosen for the service of the Sanctuary. They belonged to it, not only as worshippers, but were permanently occupied there. They were selected for the service of God, in lieu of all the first-born of Israel, who were to be consecrated to God in acknowledgment that they had received all things from him, and to commemorate the slaying of the first-born in Egypt. They were located next to the Taber-

4   1.   1   15
12 &
5
3. 2   1!. 2

nacle on two sides and in the rear. They were charged with the transportation of the Tabernacle and the keeping of the sacred vessels. Moses, Aaron, and his sons, encamped in front of the Tabernacle. They were allowed a still nearer approach to God. The priests were admitted into the Holy Place, and the High Priest once a year entered the Holy of Holies. There was, then, a gradation in the sanctity of the people, corresponding to the apartments themselves. The Priesthood was not a caste, but was chosen "from among the people" by God and invested with the office which originally belonged to all the people. God promised to make them all kings and priests. Ex. 19: 6. This is the destiny of God's people. They were not at first ready for the full realization of this promise. They showed, by defalcation and disorders, that they could not yet rule themselves. This right to reign was therefore left in abeyance for a time. The *kingly* authority was temporarily committed to one of their number, (Deut. 17: 15;) to one who had no claim to it, in anticipation of the full realization of the promise. This is so also in the Priesthood. The Priest is one who enjoys a degree of intercourse with God which is denied to others. He comes nearer to God. Heb. 5: 1. The characteristic expression is that they *come* near to God, and *bring* near the appointed offerings. Israel was a nation of Priests, but was not yet ripe for the office. They showed this at Mount Sinai. They trembled at the presence of God and entreated Him not to come near them, but speak through Moses. This was a confession of their unfitness to approach God, but the Priestly office was not to be abandoned; it was put into the hands of a few as representatives, until the time when all should be priests.

The *Levites* had no inheritance. The Lord was their inheritance. Their labor was given exclusively to Him. No other labor was allowed them. The Lord gave them their support from the Sanctuary. Forty-eight cities, four in each tribe, with their suburbs, were assigned them in the territory of the several tribes. Six of them were *Cities of Refuge*. These cities were counted as belonging to the tribes in which they were situated. The

Levites were thus distributed among the people. These six Cities of Refuge—three on each side of the Jordan—were sanctuaries or asylums not for criminals but to protect the unintentional manslayer. 1 Kings, 2: 26. As the altar was the place of refuge, so were these cities. The manslayer was to remain there till the death of the High Priest. Num. 35: 25; Josh. 20: 6. There are various explanations of this.

1. Some think that the death of the High Priest was so great a public calamity, that all private feelings of grief and revenge should be obliterated. 2. Others think that the Cities of Refuge were under the special control of the High Priest, and his control being ended at his death, they became free. 3. The true view is, that the High Priest being the representative of the whole people, his death had a peculiar expiatory force, and set the man free from his disabilities. . This was typical of Christ.

The Support of the Levites.—Num. 18: 21-32. There was no tribute paid by the people directly to the Levites, but *one-tenth* was given to God. Ten was the complete number of the digits, and hence represented the total amount of their possessions. One part was given to God in acknowledgment that the whole came from Him. Gen. 28: 22. This tithe was given to the Levites, and they in turn gave *one-tenth* of what they received to the Lord, and this was bestowed upon the priests. Lev. 23: 9. The first fruits of the harvest were presented to the Lord and given to the priests; also the firstlings of cattle; also the first-born of men were to be redeemed and the sum obtained given to the priests. This furnished ample support for the Levites. They had no landed estates. They were dependent upon the rigorous observance of the Law by the people. They were to attend to the service of the Sanctuary from the age of 25 or 30, to 50—in the prime of life. The *Priests* must be without blemish in their persons. They might eat of the sacred things, but could not offer at the altar, unless free from impurity.

DRESS.—The ordinary dress of the priests consisted of *fine white linen*; namely, the mitre, robe, cloak, &c.

Ex. 28. They wore a cap, breeches, and a cloak reaching from the neck to the feet. These represented purity and holiness. This appears: (1.) They were called "holy garments." Ex. 28 : 4. (2.) In Rev. 18 : 8, 13, 14, the same dress is repeatedly spoken of as worn by angels; Mark 16 : 5. Also worn by "the ancient of days." Dan. 7 : 9.

The *Girdle* was made of fine linen ornamented with blue, purple and scarlet. The High Priest's dress was distinguished by its elegance and costliness. He wore the same style of dress as the ordinary priest, but over it he wore a robe of blue woven in one piece. It was thus seamless, like the robe of our Saviour, signifying completeness or perfection. Blue is the color of the heavens, indicating the celestial character of the wearer.

The *Ephod* was in two pieces, back and front, joined by clasps on the shoulders. The clasps were made of onyx, on which were graven the names of the tribes. It was made of fine linen, ornamented with gold, blue, purple and scarlet. These were the colors of a gorgeous sky and of the inner coverings of the Tabernacle. They denoted the divine or heavenly functions of the wearer.

The *Breastplate* was over the Ephod—was made of linen in a square piece, and was adorned with gold, blue, purple and scarlet. In it were twelve precious stones in four rows; on each stone was the name of a tribe. The material of the Breastplate was folded so as to make a pouch, to contain the Urim and Thummim, which signified respectively *light* and *perfection*. These terms are nowhere explained. The *Breastplate* was attached to the Ephod by chains and rings. Ex. 28 : 28. The High Priest thus bore the names of the tribes conspicuously on his person, when he approached the Lord, signifying that he appeared as the representative of the people. The stones were all precious but different, signifying that God's people have their distinctive peculiarities.

The *Urim and Thummim* were worn when the High Priest approached God to ask counsel,—signifying the divine infallibility, etc.

The *Mitre* was of linen, like that of the ordinary priests but differed in form—probably being higher—and had a golden plate on the forehead, bearing the inscription—" HOLINESS TO THE LORD." No mention is made of a covering for the feet, whence it appears that they went unshod, as, e. g., Moses on Mt. Sinai, and Joshua in the presence of the captain of the Lord's hosts. Shoes were to protect the feet from defilement. Those who were in the Tabernacle were on holy ground, where nothing was needed for the feet. The idea is that purity was required of those who came near to God.

The sacredness attached to the Priests and Levites was conveyed to them by the rites of consecration. Israel was originally constituted the people of God by a solemn service. It was after the proclamation of the Law from Sinai, Ex. Chapters 20 and 23. The people promised obedience. It was before the Tabernacle was made or any ordinance of worship established. To conclude this covenant, an Altar was erected as a point of meeting, around which were 12 pillars. So the place where God revealed himself was in the midst of the people. Moses who acted as Priest, took the blood, and sprinkled half on the *Altar*, and half on the people. This was done after the reading of the law, and the people had promised obedience. There was no sin-offering on this occasion, because the law of the sin-offering was not yet promulgated. The Patriarchal sacrifice was still in use. The burnt-offering, which was the primitive form, stands here as sufficient for expiation. The sprinkling of blood was designed to express expiation for sin. The peculiarity of this sacrifice was that one-half of the blood was placed on the altar, signifying God's acceptance of his part of his covenant; and one-half on the people, denoting the application of its merits to those for whom it was shed. Some have thought that an additional reason was, that it was a satisfaction of a covenant, and the blood was divided between the two contracting parties, as was sometimes customary.

It indicated that both would be united in life and purpose henceforth. The slaying of the victim denoted the judgment which would follow the breakers of the covenant. After this was the *Sacrificial Meal*. The people were represented by Moses, Aaron and his sons, and the 70 elders. *Seventy* was a *symbolical* number. It was

the product of 7 and 10—the latter denoting completeness. It was also a *historical* number, being the number of Jacob's descendants, when he went down to Egypt, Gen. 46: 27. It was also the number of Noah's descendants, Gen. 10. The number represented a world-wide function and destiny. These representatives of the people went up and saw God in Mt. Sinai, and ate and drank before him. The people were then brought into communion with God, and became his peculiar people. This relation was to be permanently maintained and expressed by the service of the Sanctuary.

The *Consecration of the Priests.*—Lev. 8. Effected by two series of equivalent acts of three each. The *first* series was symbolical, and the *second*, sacrificial.

The *first* series consisted of (1) *Washing*, which denoted preliminary cleansing; (2) *Clothing*, which denoted investiture with the priestly office; (3) *Anointing*, which denoted the imparting of the Holy Spirit.

The *second* series consisted of (1) *Sin*-offering, which purged from sin, and corresponded to the washing; (2) *Burnt*-offering, which denoted consecration to sacred office, and corresponded to the clothing; (3) *Peace*-offering, which sealed communion with God, and corresponded to the anointing.

Moses officiated in the sacrifices because there were no Priests yet; for Aaron and his sons were not properly priests until the service was over. *Blood* was put on the tip of the ear, right thumb, and right great toe, to make atonement for guilt and purify these organs for God's service. Their persons and dress were also sprinkled with blood and oil. These services were repeated for seven days, and on the eighth day began their sacred functions. During those first seven days, they were not to leave the court of the Tabernacle. These services were to be repeated whenever a new High Priest was to be consecrated.

The *Consecration of the Levites* is described in Numbers 8: 5-22. This took place when they left Mt. Sinai, because their part of the services was to transport the Tabernacle, and there was thus a necessity for them. The rites of consecration were inferior in solemnity to the consecration of the priests. Moses was directed to *cleanse* the *Levites*, but to *sanctify* the *Priests*. There were two series of acts and two in each.

The *first* series, symbolical as before, consisted of (1) Washing and Cleansing; (2) Consecration by Waving. The *second* series was sacrificial. (1) Sin-offering; (2) Burnt-offering. In the cleansing they were sprinkled with the water of purifying. Their hair was shaven and clothes washed. Their clothes were renewed and cleansed, because they were to enter upon a new function. They had no official dress, since they only attended the priests, and were not really invested with office. They were substitutes for the first-born of all the tribes. The children of Israel laid their hands on the Levites, and the obligation of service was thereby transferred to them. Then the Levites were waved toward the Tabernacle and toward the Priests, denoting that they were given to the latter to perform the service of the sanctuary. The sacrificial acts were (1) Sin-offering, which denoted purgation of sin, and (2) *Burnt*-offering, which denoted consecration. They were then prepared for the service of the Tabernacle, to which they were set apart.

LECTURE X.

Sacred Times.

The most general term is Moadhim, set times, because they returned at stated periods. The general idea is that of certain portions of time withdrawn from their ordinary occupations, and devoted to God; yet not as a *payment*, but as a tribute, and an acknowledgment that all their time belonged to God and His service.

These special duties were (a) *Negative*, i. e., abstinence from ordinary secular labor; (b) *Positive*, i. e., special acts of worship, both ceremonial and spiritual, as the multiplication of sacrifices and holy convocations, prayer and religious devotions.

The *Sacred Seasons* instituted by Moses, were of three kinds, contemplating God under three aspects, as 1. *Creator;* 2. *Preserver;* 3. *Sanctifier.*

I. As *Creator.* A series of Sabbaths, or *Sabbatical Series*, based on the weekly Sabbath, being the same idea extended. The Sabbath had existed from the beginning of the world, just as the sacrifice had from the *Fall*. Both these primitive institutions were incorporated and expanded in the Mosaic Ritual. That the Sabbath was so instituted at the beginning of the world appears—

(1) From Gen. 2 : 3. This could not have been inserted in the account by way of anticipation of a *future* Sabbath, because God's blessing the *seventh* day could no more be postponed than His blessing the other days of creation.

(2) From the actual allusions before Sinai, to periods of seven days, and the sacredness of the number *seven*. There were *seven* clean animals in the Ark; and Noah waited *seven* days at different times. It was incorporated in the language :—the verb *to swear*, in Hebrew, is derived from the word seven.

(3) These periods of seven days, and the sacredness of the number seven, can be traced to other nations who did not borrow from the Jews.

(4) The *Sabbath* was observed before *Sinai* by the children of Israel. Ex. 12: 19.

(5) In the Fourth Commandment the word *remember* occurs.

The Sabbatical Series was formed by applying the number *seven* to every denomination of time. The seventh *day* was the *Sabbath* ;—a day of rest for *man* and *beast*. The seventh *year* was a year of rest for the *land*, which was to remain uncultivated that year. The Fifteenth year, or the year following the Seventh Sabbatical year was the *Year of Jubilee*, when took place the restoration of property, reparation for injuries, etc. The seventh *month* was in a certain sense sacred. Its first day was to be kept as a Sabbath by abstaining from labor, and there were a great number of festivals in this month. These were all intended to be remembrancers of God, and a testimony to Him who Himself rested on the seventh day of Creation. The refusing to keep the Sabbath was a denial of the Creator, and hence the Sabbath was spoken of as a sign of the covenant of God with Israel. It represented the covenant on the side of *Nature*, as circumcision did on the side of *Grace*. These various Sabbaths were periods of rest from worldly labor in commemoration of God's rest. They were designed further to remind the Israelites of the rest that God had given them from the bondage of *Egypt*. It restored man's strength, and was also a transient restoration of man's primitive condition before the curse of labor had been pronounced upon him, and furthermore was a type of the future rest from toil.

II. Those which celebrate God as *Preserver*, in two respects, viz., Historical and Agricultural. These feasts numbered three, and were

1. The *Passover*, commemorating their deliverance from Egypt and the slaying of the first-born. It was at the beginning of the harvest. It was on the fifteenth day of the first month, (i. e., the day following the fourteenth day,) and lasted for seven days.

2. The Feast of *Weeks* or *Pentecost*, occurring on the fiftieth day after the Passover, lasting *one* day only. This feast marked the end of the harvest. The Feast of *Weeks*, according to tradition, commemorated the giving of the Law.

3. The Feast of *Tabernacles*, on the fifteenth day of the seventh month, and lasted seven days. It commemorated the dwelling in tents in the wilderness. It also marked the end of the vintage, or the ingathering of fruits.

The feasts of the Passover and Tabernacles began at full moon. After the feast of Tabernacles was the day of the Solemn Assembly, a general and formal conclusion of all the festivals of the year.

III. Those in which God is regarded as a *Sanctifier*. This class contained one item, the great Day of Atonement. It was a general expiation for the sins of the year. It occurred on the tenth day of the seventh month.

There were seven days in the year which were *festive* Sabbaths, besides the weekly Sabbaths. These were the first and seventh days of the Passover, the day of the Feast of Weeks, and four days in the sacred (i. e., the seventh) month. These last were the first, the tenth (i. e. day of atonement,) the fifteenth (i. e., the first day of the Feast of Tabernacles,) and the twenty-second (i. e., the day after the Feast of Tabernacles.) All these were to be observed as Sabbaths by abstinence from labor, &c.

These various sacred times had their special sacrificial services. On every day, a lamb was offered, morning and evening, for a burnt-offering, together with the appropriate meat-offering. On the weekly Sabbath, the daily Sacrifices were doubled and fresh, Shew Bread was to be put on the Table. On the first day of each *month*, there was a festival-offering of a *he-goat* for a Sin-offering, and ten animals, viz., two bullocks, one ram and seven lambs of the first year, for a burnt-offering. No abstinence from labor was enjoined, but a trumpet was blown, (Num. 10 : 10) which represented the loud call to God by the people that He would remember them. The first day of the seventh month was to be kept as a Sabbath, and a double festival-offering was to be presented. Abstinence from labor was enjoined, and the trumpet was sounded, in louder tones.

I. The *Passover* was instituted when they left Egypt, and was to be observed annually thenceforth. It was called also the Feast of Unleavened Bread. It consisted of two parts. (a) the Passover Meal strictly so called ; (b) the eating of unleavened bread for seven days. The Passover is to be reckoned a *sacrifice*. Some of the Reformed Theologians deny this in order to confute the Romanists who said that the Lord's Supper was a sacrifice, because the passover which it supplanted was such. That it was a sacrifice appears

(1) Because it was expressly so called. Ex. 12 : 27 ; I. Cor. 5 : 7. (2) It was so regarded by the Jews, although the blood was not sprinkled on the altar at first, (Deut. 16 : 5–7) because the Tabernacle was not yet built. It *was* offered there and the blood sprinkled on the altar in later times. II. Chron. 30 : 16; 35 : 11. The Pass-

over was not a *Sin*-offering. It had none of the latter's peculiar features, but its blood had an atoning virtue. It was a species of *Peace*-offering. It included a Sacrificial Meal.

The requirements were exact. The *lamb* was to be selected on the tenth day, i. e., *four* days previous to the feast. This was fancifully supposed to represent the four generations of Israel in Egypt, (Gen. 15 : 16,) while others supposed it to have reference to the symbolical character of the number four. Both explanations are too remote. It was probably set apart on the tenth day for the same reason that the great Day of Atonement was on the tenth day. Notice the Ten Commandments and the ten plagues, etc. It occurs frequently, and besides being convenient, is symbolical of completeness. The lamb was to be slain *between the evenings*, where the original does not use the Dual, and which may mean (a) between the sunset of the first day and the total darkness of the second ; or (b) from the latter part of the afternoon till sunset. This is the correct view, as may be shown. In the *first* place, the blood was to be sprinkled on the door posts and lintels of the house. Atonement was thus made for the house and its occupant. The head of the family exercised this priestly function, which was afterward confined to the priests.

The Passover Meal denoted communion with God, based on the expiation of sin.

Peculiarities of this Feast.—The lamb must be placed upon the table *whole*. No bones were to be broken. It was typical of Christ's body, and the unity of His church and people. The whole lamb was to be eaten in one house. The same idea was included as before. None must be left until the next day. It must not be boiled, which would separate it, but was to be roasted, to preserve its oneness. No part of it was to be carried out of the house. All that remained was to be burned, to protect it from corruption or contact with common things.

The *manner* of eating it was designed to remind them of their previous condition, and of the circumstances of its institution and the great deliverance which it commemorated. It was to be eaten with bitter herbs, which

suggested the bitterness of Egyptian oppression, and with unleavened bread, which was a symbolical representation of incorruption, and which had also an historical association, because they had not time to leaven their bread. Deut. 16 : 3. It was to be eaten in haste, with their loins girded, and shoes on their feet, and staves in their hands. These peculiar circumstances were laid aside in later times. During each of these seven days, a goat was to be offered for a sin-offering, and, in addition, ten animals, viz., 2 bullocks, 1 ram, and 7 lambs, for a burnt offering, and the prescribed meat-offering. A sheaf of the first-fruits was to be waved before the Lord, before they could partake of the harvest. Lev. 23 : 10.

II. The *Feast of Weeks.*—Fifty days after the second day of the *Passover,* i. e., the day following the completion of seven weeks. It was called also the *Feast of Harvest.* Ex. 23 : 16 ; The day of First Fruits ; and was called Pentecost in Josephus and in the New Testament, Acts 2 : 1. Barley harvest began at the time of the Passover, and wheat harvest ended with the Feast of Weeks. This feast lasted one day, which day possessed a Sabbatic character. No work was to be done ; and a holy convocation was enjoined. Two loaves of the first fruits and the usual festive offering, viz., a he-goat for the sin-offering, and ten animals for the burnt-offering, consisting of 2 bullocks, 1 ram, and 7 lambs—and the customary meat-offering. Now that the harvest was concluded, *loaves* and not *sheaves*, were to be brought, just as at the Passover. *Two loaves* were now brought, representing a livelier sense of gratitude at the end of the feast.

III. *The Feast of Tabernacles,* called also the *Feast* of *Ingathering,* was held after the fruits were gathered in, particularly the oil and wine. It was celebrated for seven days, beginning with the 15th day of the 7th month. They were to dwell in booths, commemorating their sojourn in the wilderness. It thus had both historical and agricultural associations. It was the most joyous feast of the year. The *offerings* were larger than on the other occasions, consisting of *two* rams, *fourteen* lambs, and *thirteen* bullocks at the beginning, and seven at the close. The number decreased *one* each day, making 70 in all.

The first day was observed as a Sabbath, and then the *eighth* day, or the day after the festival, which did not belong strictly to the feast. That this is so appears, (1) because the lodging in the booths lasted only *seven* days; and (2) because the sacrifices on this day did not stand in regular gradation to those of the other days, but consisted of *ten* animals, viz., *one* he-goat, *one* bullock, *one* ram, and *seven* lambs. This was a solemn termination of all the festivals of the year.

The Great Day of Atonement.—This occurred five days before the feast of *Tabernacles*, on the *tenth* day of the *seventh* month. It represented a general atonement for the sins of Israel during the year, and for the sanctuary itself; Lev. 16 : 16. The atonement on this day was not merely for undiscovered sins, because these were included in the general atonement at the new moon, but all the sins of the year were atoned for afresh. This was an intimation that the acts of atonement were incomplete, as indicated in the Epistle to the Hebrews. This was not merely to *supplement* the previous sacrifices or atonement, but it was the *same act*. It was made in the Holy of Holies by the High Priest, and was thus a fuller and more exalted type of Christ, the *true* and *adequate* atonement. The entire day was observed as a *fast*, the only fast of divine appointment in the Jewish Calendar. Then came the special services of the day. The High Priest first bathed himself and put on a clean white garment, i. e., the ordinary dress of the priests and not his usual robe. After making a *Sin* and *Burnt*-offering for himself and his house, came the characteristic service of the day—an offering of *two he-goats* and a *ram* for a burnt-offering. The atonement was made in the Holy of Holies. God appeared in a cloud over the Mercy-seat, and the blood of the sin-offering of the priests and of the sin-offering of the people was sprinkled upon the Mercy-seat. This expiation was repeated at the Altar of Incense and at the Brazen Altar in the Court. The most remarkable peculiarity was in the fact that there were *two* he-goats in the sin-offering. One was slain, and its blood was carried into the Holy of Holies. The other was sent into the wilderness. Lots were first cast upon

them, one for Jehovah, (LA-JEHOVAH) and one for (LA-AZAZEL,) a word derived from AZAL, to remove.
Four explanations of this term.
1. As a *place;*
2. As the *name* of the goat;
3. As an *abstract term;*
4. As a personal *being.*

I. If a *place*, it must be either the proper name of some particular locality in the wilderness to which the goat was to be taken, or a remote retired place. There is no trace anywhere of such a name or place. In Lev. 16: 10, he was to be taken into the wilderness.

II. The English version and the Vulgate apply this term to the *goat*, and render it "*Scape-goat.*" Some say it is a compound word, from E Z, a goat, and that AZAL, means to go away. This is not true, but a fanciful explanation. It may mean something entirely removed. One name was given to Jehovah, and one LA-AZAZEL.

III. If it was an *abstract* term, it must have represented a complete removal, and explained the two ideas in the pardon of sin,—(a) expiation, (b) removal. The ordinary sacrifice was sufficient to express the former, but, in this case, both ideas must be represented; *first*, a goat was to be slain as an expiation, and, *secondly*, the sins were to be carried away by the other goat.

IV. Those who adopt this view say it was a *personal designation*, a name for *Satan*. They argue (1) that it makes a more exact contrast in the lots, as *God* in contradistinction to *Satan*. (2) That this goat was sent to *Azazel*, in the wilderness, and that in several passages of Scripture the wilderness is represented as the especial abode of devils and evil spirits; Isa. 13: 21; 34: 14. The word translated *Satyr* is translated *Devils* in Lev. 17: 7, and in Rev. 18: 2. Devils are spoken of as inhabiting waste places. In Matth. 12: 43, the evil spirit is spoken of as walking through dry places. In Luke 8: 27, we read that an evil spirit was in the tombs. Also in the Apocrypha; Tobit 8: 3; Baruch 4: 35. (3) The name Azazel, they say, is appropriate for Satan, as being utterly *removed* from the presence of God. The difficulties of this personal view are (a) Satan is nowhere else in the Bible called by this name. (b) There is no allusion to Satan as connected with the Day of Atonement. There is nothing in the *Ceremonial* to suggest this view, unless it be the doubtful meaning of this word. Many in modern times adopt this view, on this supposition.

If *Azazel* is Satan, it is variously explained in *four ways*.

(1.) That the goat was sent as a sacrifice to propitiate the Devil. To this we say: (a) This idea is abhorrent to the notions of religion and to the Mosaic institutions, which particularly forbade the worship of anything but God,—and expressly prohibited sacrifice to Devils; Lev. 17:7. (b) The *two* goats were *one* offering and not *two*; and were also a *Sin*-offering, which could not have been appropriately offered to the Devil, because it implied holiness in the person to whom it was offered. Both the goats were brought to the Tabernacle, and God decided which was to be sent into the wilderness. The only reason why there were two animals was because two ideas were to be represented; one must be alive to carry away the sin after the other had been sacrificed. The second goat was really the first one over again, being analogous to the two birds in the cleansing of the leper.

(2.) That the Goat, laden with the sins of the people, was sent to the Devil to be tormented by him, and to show God's hatred of sin. There is nothing to substantiate this view.

(3.) That the sins belonged to the Devil and hence were sent there in the person of the goat.

(4.) This is the most common explanation, that it was an act of defiance and scorn against the *Devil*, the seducer and accuser of Mankind. The sins are sent to the Devil, having been first atoned for, that he may do his worst with them. He can never bring Israel into condemnation.

The choice seems to be between this last view and the view which makes it an *abstract* idea. It would seem that the latter is preferable. It appears that the two goats are identical in signification, one supplementing the other,—the second carrying out what the first could not do.

All *typical* theories which make a distinction between the two goats are erroneous.

(1.) Prof. Bush says that the first goat represents Christ, and the second the Jews.

(2.) Some hold that the first goat represented Christ's human nature, and the second his divine nature.

(3.) Or that the first represented Christ's death, and the second his resurrection.

Christ accomplished both ideas, and hence both were typical of Christ, the first making atonement for, and the second securing the removal of sin. After this, the High Priest removed his dress, washed himself, put on his official robes, and then offered the proper offerings. The person who took the goat into the wilderness, and the one who burned the fat of the sin-offering, were both rendered unclean.

LECTURES IN PHILOLOGY.

LECTURE I.

THE FAMILIES OF LANGUAGES.

Gen. 11 : 1—" And the whole earth was of one language, and of one speech:" and so it was originally.

This verse has been a stimulus to endeavors to find this primitive tongue. The test of having found it would be to show clearly that all others owe their origin to and are derived from it. All research, however, has thus far shown that at this day it is too late to discover it. But though such is the case, yet astonishing analogies have been discovered.

Research formerly proceeded on several erroneous assumptions :—e. g.,

1. It was assumed that a bare similarity of sound between words of like sense denoted identity of origin. But this is not so; while, on the other hand, sounds and words originally alike must be so much changed as not to be recognized. The modern Greek *uατι* (I) and the Polynesian *mata* (I) have no connection of origin. On the other hand, *journey* comes from *dies*, through *diurnus* and the French *jour*. So also *stranger*.

2. It was assumed that the presence of the same or related words in two languages, established their *organic* connection. But such words may have been merely *borrowed* from one language by another by

intercourse;—e. g., Moslem, Sultan, Dragoman, are from the Arabic, and yet the English has no connection with it.

3. They paid attention only to the etymology of the words, disregarding the grammatical structure of the language, which is a truer test. Though the English has words from many languages, its grammatical structure clearly denotes its origin, the Anglo-Saxon, Germanic. The Turkish, the Persian, the Hindoo languages are entirely distinct from the Arabic, and though they are full of words borrowed from the Arabic,, their grammatical structure clearly shows their distinctness.

4. It was assumed that relationship between two languages proved that one was derived from the other: whereas both may have been derived from some other language. Latin is related to Greek; both are related to Sanscrit; yet neither has sprung from the other. There is only an affinity.

Now that sounder principles have been adopted, although unity of language has not been and probably cannot be reached, yet astonishing analogies have been discovered, and languages have been reduced to a few Groups. Ethnology aids here, though its divisions and those of Philology do not *precisely* coincide. There are nations closely allied by physical structure, which speak languages entirely distinct, and *vice versa*. Hence existing diversity of both are not inconsistent with unity of origin.

The Old Testament is written in Hebrew, (with a few verses in Chaldee). This language was not selected because of any special sacredness, or because it was the primitive language: but merely because it was the language spoken by the people chosen as the custodians of revelation during the time the revelation was being given.

There are eight great Families of Languages, including almost all. Some few have not yet been classified; e. g., the Basque language, near the Bay of Biscay, in France, has no apparent affinity to any language. Many have not yet been thoroughly examined. But enough is known to justify the foregoing classification. These eight Families differ not only in their stock of *words*, but also in their *general structure*, and are thus divided into three great Groups.

I. *Isolating Languages*, or those of undeveloped roots : having no inflection ; no parts of speech ; no modifications of the forms of words to express number, gender, tense, etc. ; and no derivation of words from one another ; but only ultimate roots thrown together.

II. *Agglutinative Languages* :—One step better ; not having mere ultimate roots loosely thrown together, but possessing all the various parts of speech, gender, number, etc., by modifying syllables ; though these are only artificially cemented to the root, and do not lose their individuality. The word is built up by additions, the original and independent character of its constituents not however being lost sight of.

III. *Inflective Languages*:—most highly developed ; the word not being a mere conglomeration, but an organic whole. It is a growth, in which the branches are inseparably joined to the trunk.

    I. Includes 3 families.
    II.   "   3   "
    III.   "   2   "

We will glance at all these families. For details see Dwight's Philology,—Max Muller,—Whitney, etc.

I. ISOLATING GROUP.

First Family,—Malay or *Polynesian*. This extends over Malacca and the great body of islands in the Indian and Pacific oceans from Madagascar to the Sandwich Islands.

Polysyllabic ; restricted in the number of sounds ; has from seven to ten consonants. Each word is a simple syllable, i. e., a vowel, or a consonant and vowel. A mixed syllable, or a final, or compound consonant is unknown.

Second Family,—Chinese. This extends over S. E. Asia, China proper, farther India, Thibet, Birmah, Siam.

Monosyllabic ; words have no determinate value as parts of speech ; the same word may be a verb, and an adjective, and a noun, etc. There is no inflection for gender, except personal pronouns, which have a peculiar variation for number, by fusion with numerals, forming a singular, dual, triple and plural. The Pronoun of the First Person has a variation, according as the speaker is included or not. This is the purest type of Isolating Languages ; the most improtant ; the best known ; the most highly cultivated ; has a large and extensive literature.

Third Family,—Hamitic, Coptic, or Ancient Egyptian. This is separated from the other families of the group by the entire continent of Asia. It is spoken also in Abyssinia, and among the Libyan tribes, as well as among the Hottentots, and the Bushmen of South Africa.

Monosyllabic ; consists of mere roots ; has a slight approach to inflection ; has syllabic suffixes.

See the hieroglyphics, mummy wrappings, etc. This language ceased to be spoken in Egypt three or four centuries ago.

II. AGGLUTINATIVE GROUP.

First Family. This is the most important Group—Turanian or Scythian. Includes the roving tribes of Central and Northern Asia, and along the north of Europe; consisting of Mongolians, Tartars, Fins, Laplanders, Turks, Southern Hindostanee, Japanese.

The root is always at the beginning of the word, *agglutinative ;* the syllables being always *suffixed.*

Second Family,—South African. All Southern Africa, from a few degrees north of the Equator, with the exception of the Hottentots and Bushmen.

All the languages of this Family are closely related, the West and East Coast of Africa being much alike. Though spoken by barbarous tribes, yet it has great flexibility of structure and copiousness of form. It has a series of conjugations much like the Hebrew. The agglutinative syllables are often *prefixed.* There is no declension of nouns, etc.

Third Family,—-American. North American Indians. It has an immense variety of dialects, yet all are related.

Polysynthetic or incorporative; accumulates words of enormous length. Pronouns and numerals have from *three* to *ten* syllables.

III. INFLECTIVE GROUP.

Two Families,—spoken by the white race, and the most influential. It is spoken by civilized nations, and is therefore best known.

(1.) *Indo-European.*
(2.) *Semitic.*

The New Testament is written in the former; the Old Testament in the latter. The Indo-European is so called from the extremes of territory where it is spoken—India and Europe. We find a belt ex-

tending between them through Afghanistan, Persia, Europe, (excepting in the north of Europe.)

DIFFERENCES BETWEEN THE TWO FAMILIES:

Indo-European tongues form words and inflections by additions external to the root ; Semitic by internal changes mainly. E. g. :
Love—lover—loving—beloved.
Amo—amor—amatus—amabilis.
קָטֹל—קְטָל־—קָטַל—קְטַל־—etc.
The Semitic is formed by *vowel* changes in the body of the root, or prefixed or affixed ; or else by doubling the letters of the root, (except in pronominal suffixes.)

In the Indo-European, formative prefixes, etc., are outside ; the root only changes through laws of, *euphony*, as cædo, cæsus, incido, in order to ease the pronunciation. Some internal changes have now a signification which they did not originally possess ; e. g., man, men ; foot, feet ; break, broke. These *look* like internal inflection, but are not so. *Man* had a regular plural, *mans*,—the change of *a* to *e* being merely euphonic, and often occurring in the singular.

The Indo-European root is a single syllable, the ultimate unit of articulate speech ; a vowel, or a vowel with one or more associated consonants. The root is one indivisible, invariable whole, the vowel being an inalienable part of it. The Semitic roots have only consonants, and as a root is unpronounceable, being a frame-work or skeleton, while the vowels are the tissue and flesh. Consonants determine the *radical* signification of the word which the vowels *shade* or *alter*. The Semitic alphabet has no vowels ; the Indo-European languages, in which vowels form an essential part, in adopting the Semitic alphabet, changed the superabundant guttural into vowels, e. g., א=α, a ; ח=ε, e ; ה=η, a ; י=o.

There is no fixed number of letters in the Indo-European roots, but they must be pronounced in one *syllable*. The Semitic has a uniform number; biliterals are too brief, and triliterals are the briefest that could give a sufficient number of combinations. Therefore Semitic words are *triliteral*. Quadriliterals are a later formation.

LECTURE II.

(1.) It is hence easier for the Semitic verb to have its peculiarities than for the Indo-European verb. The verb in Semitic is the word *par excellence*, giving life to every sentence. It has the simplest vowels, as Kamets, etc., especially in the Arabic. It intensifies the meaning and pronunciation by doubling the radicals. The verb has fewer peculiarities in the Indo-European. Causatives, desideratives, etc., correspond in *some* degree to the Semitic inflections.

(2.) Hence there is a richness in the Indo-European inflections, and more variety is possible ; poverty in the Semitic as to tense, mood, etc. Greek has nine tenses ; Semitic two. Unlimited means in Indo-European of multiplying them ; but the changes of vowels possible in the three consonants of the Semitic, are few. The Semitic noun in the construct state, results from the same fundamental principle.

The Indo-European great variety of tongues,— Celtic, Germanic, Italic, Sclavonic, Greek, Iranian, Indian. The Semitic has only three branches—Aramæan Hebrew, and Arabic, all closely related.

(3.) The Semitic has been of a stationary character from its very formation ; the Indo-European has more mobility. The former is rigid and changes slowly. From Moses to Malachi, (1,000 years,) there appears less change than in the English since Shakespeare, (300 years), while 1,000 years back, in the time of Alfred, the Saxon language was used, and the English was still unformed. The Indo-European is perpetually developing and progressing. The Semitic structure does not admit of this—and this reacted on the nations speaking it. The Semite is the same from age to age ; has the same habits and modes of life, The Semite remains in the same place ; the Indo-European stretches over both of the continents of Europe and Asia. For this reason, the Old Testament was given to the Semite, to remain and keep the oracles of God. But when Christ came, and the Gospel was aggressive, and to be spread, then the New Testament was given in an Indo-European tongue.

The lack of variety in the Semitic tongues is due not only to their method of internal *flection*, but also to their triliteral roots, No attrition of consonants at ends of words is possible, for the word can't spare any, without changing itself entirely ; no abridging ; no changing of the three consonants. The Arabic has now many roots which are the same as those used by Moses.

The stationary character of the people reacted on the language, as seen in the fact that there is no need of new terms, and their own language was not imposed by conquest and commerce on new nations, or corrupted and mixed thereby, as is seen in the English. Arabic is now left alone to represent the family.

The *Second great Difference*, (relating to the meaning, not to the outward form,) is that *the Semitic is more pictorial; the Indo-European is more reflective.*

E. g., (1.) Semitic has only two genders : the idea of sex being carried through all inanimate nature and abstractions. Indo-European languages almost all have a third gender for objects destitute of sex, though not always regarding it.

(2.) While, in both languages, words denoting abstractions are based on roots primarily relating to external objects, in Indo-European this primary idea is lost sight of, in Semitic it is retained. As *sincere, sine cera*—pure honey ; *tribulation, tribulum*, a threshing instrument ; *agony*, referring to the *struggles* of the contestants in games. *Inculcate, tread* grain *into* the soil. In Semitic the metaphor remains in consciousness ; both significations co-exist. *Anger*, אַף, אָנַף, to breathe, hard breathing ; חֵמָה, heat ; חָרוֹן, burning ; יָעַ, boiling ; גָּנַי, breaking asunder ; רָעַם, roaring. *Desire*, צָבָא, thirst ; כָּסַף, grow pale. *Pardon*, כָּפַר, cover ; כָּסָה, hide. *Patient*, slow breathing ; *impatient*, fast breathing.

(3.) A want of precision, or definiteness of expression. Their pictorial form of expression barely suggests the thought in outline. It aims at vividness and force more than detail. Thus the Semitic (in the *tenses*) refers all to the unlimited *past* or the unlimited *future*, and has only one form of each. The Indo-European adds the vanishing *present*, and to the other various modifications, adds the imperfect, perfect, pluperfect, future, and future perfect. So of *moods*.

The Semitic gives the sentences without concatenation, without denoting their relation, and has few conjunctions. It simply joins two clauses by the word *and*, leaving the reader to guess at the nature of the connection. The Indo-European has a multitude of particles, etc.

(4.) Range and description of their literatures. The Semitic writes of history (or palpable facts,) tales, fables, parables (or imaginative fiction,) lyric and sententious poetry, brief utterances of the feelings or wise sayings. But it has no romances proper, no heroic or dramatic poems with complicated plots. It has no orations of such a kind as those of Webster and Calhoun ; and no arguments advancing to an irresistible conclusion.

Renan, taking up the idea, says the Semites were *monotheists* by instinct ; but he takes no notice of the idolatrous Assyrians and Ninevites, who were Semites.

Hence the Semitic was especially fitted for the Old Testament, dealing in outlines and shadows. The New Testament is precise and clearly revealed, and therefore in its final form, required an Indo-European tongue. Paul was educated in Grecian philosophy, etc.

The Third Difference is a subordinate one, *The mode of writing.* The Semite writes from right to left ; the Indo-European the reverse. (Exceptions to both are found. The Ethiopic from left to right like the Greek ; Persian, Hindoo, from right to left like the Arabic.)

POINTS OF AGREEMENT.

They belong to the same Group, the Inflective, and have, therefore, (1) many grammatical analogies ; (2) a great number of roots clearly identical. For examples, see Gesenius. (Though many similar sounds are merely casual ; e. g., באר, well, and the English *bore* are not related ; nor are דרך and *direction ;* nor natural sounds קרא, *cry ;* אב, *pa, pater.*)

Some say all triliteral roots were originally biliteral, and that the triliterals were formed by inserting weak letters, or adding letters: גז to cut, גזר—to off—גזע to cut down—גזל to flay—גזז to shear—גזה to hew—גזם to devour—גזר to separate—גזע to pass through, etc.

The name given to the family of languages kindred to Hebrew and Chaldee, have been many. Jerome called them "*oriental*," but we know of countries farther east, where the Semitic prevails: "*Syro-Arabian*," (named from the extreme limits, just as Indo-European;) *Semitic*," (from Shem) is the name most used, for (Gen. 10,) Shemites are the chief member of the group. The Hebrew, Aramæic and Arabic languages, come from Shem; the Elamites and Libyans are also from Shem, though these speak Indo-European. Canaanites and Phœnicians are from Ham, yet they speak the Semitic languages.

The Semitic tongue extends from the Red Sea and the Mediterranean, to the Persian Gulf and Tigris, and from Mt. Taurus on the North, to the southern extremity of the Arabian Peninsula.

It includes Arabia, Palestine, Syria, and Mesopotamia. These tongues existed here as far back as they can be traced, and whenever driven hence, They are spoken there yet, though overrun by Mohammedanism.

Semitic was the language of civilization, of trade, of religion, in Ninevah, Babylon, Tyre, Judea, Judaism and Christianity arose in Palestine. The latter, though spread through the medium of Greek, yet took Semitic types of thought. Some say that parts of the N. T., as Matthew, were originally in Hebrew, but of this we cannot be certain. Mohammed took his language from Arabia. Babylon (Babel, confusion of tongues) has had a mixed population, and therefore mixed languages ever since, just as in

Constantinople to-day. Nebuchadnezzar and other monarchs were Indo-Europeans, but their generals, e. g., Robshekar, were Semites and spoke Aramæan. The name of their deity *Bel* is Semitic. Some names are partly each. On their ruins there are some Semitic characters, some Indo-European, some in a third language, perhaps Scythian.

The *Canaanites* spoke a Semitic dialect much like the Hebrew. Abraham held intercourse without an interpreter; but in Egypt Jacob's sons required one. Proper names, Melchisedec, Abimelech, Kirjath-jearim, Baal, Moloch, etc., are Semitic.

The *Phœnicians* spoke Semitic, and so also did their colonies, Carthage, and even Tarshish on the southern coast of Spain. This might arise from their nearness to Canaan. Their extensive literature has all perished. We can judge (a) from ancient authors of other languages, quoting proper names and other words. But the sound is often inadequately expressed in a foreign language, and is unreliable. (b) From Phœnician monuments; but they have no sounds, and no vowels, spacing, punctuation, etc.

(a) *Proper names* — *Tyre*, צוּר, Rock; *Carthage*, קִרְנַ הְדָשׁ, New City; *Adonis*, אֲדֹנִי, Lord; *Hannibal*, הַנִּי בַּעַל, favor of Baal; *Hasdrubal*, עֶזְרִי בַּעַל, help of Baal; *Dido*, beloved; *Cadmus*, קֶדֶם, the east, oriental.

Plautus has a passage in Carthaginian and a Latin translation.

(b) *Monuments*, as found at Malta, Marseilles, and Cadiz, have Phœnician names. The same is learned from Carthage. From Tyre we have coins, gems, votive tablets. All show that the language of the Phœnicians was like the Hebrew.

Some have said that Coptic should be classed with Semitic, as being merely an older type and a

more primitive form of it. This point is still in dispute. The argument is based on similarity of pronouns and some pronominal suffixes. But the weight of authority is against it. There are three branches of Semitic Languages:
1. *Hebraic*=Hebrew and Phœnician.
2. *Aramaic*=Chaldee, Syriac, Samaritan (mongrel).
3. *Arabic*=Arabic proper, and Ethiopic (spoken in Abyssinia).

Hebrew is intermediate, both geographically and philologically. Aramaic is north of it, Arabic south. The Arabic is the most soft, flexible and copious, the Aramaic least so. The Aramaic regular *verb* has *one vowel* (קְטַל), the Hebrew *two* (קָטַל), Arabic *three*, (קָטַל). *Conjugations* or species. The Aramaic has thirteen, eleven of which are double, thus numbering twenty-four. The Hebrew has seven, the Arabic .

The Future. The Arabic has *four* forms, the Hebrew has *three*, (simple, paragogic, and apocopated). The *Dual*. The Aramaic has none; the Hebrew only in nouns; the Arabic in nouns and verbs. Their varying copiousness is shown in vocabularies and alphabets. The Aramaic has the original twenty-two letters; the Hebrew doubles the pronunciation of one, Sin or Shin, really making twenty-three; the Arabic doubles six, making twenty-eight.

HISTORICAL ORDER.

1. Hebrew. 2. Aramæan. 3. Arabic. Hebrew is the oldest and has the oldest literature. The Arabic is the only one now in use as a *spoken* language, except among a few scattered tribes. The number of dialects of Semitic, therefore, unlike the Indo-European, is diminishing rather than increasing; the Arabic alone remains. But this does not prove

that the Arabic is the youngest and an outgrowth of the others.

Gen. 31 : 47.—Aramæan was distinct from Hebrew ; e. g., Laban gives the place mentioned an Aramæan name, Jegar-sahadutha, but Jacob gives it a Hebrew name, Gilead.

Gen. 10 ; 26.—The name Almodad has the prefix אל, the Aramaic article.

In reality Arabic is the oldest, and stands in relation to the Semitic as Sanskrit does to Indo-European. Even in the days of Moses, Hebrew had undergone more changes than Arabic had in Mahomet's time.

For purposes of comparison, Arabic is more copious and living ; Aramaic is more closely related to Hebrew.

All these languages have been and still are regarded as sacred, as Hebrew among the Jews; Aramaic or Syriac among oriental Christians ; Arabic among Mohammedans, Turks, and as in the Koran.

LECTURE III.

THE HEBREW LANGUAGE, or the original language of the Old Testament.

The Semitic family of languages included three principle branches.

1. *Aramaic*, including the *Chaldee* and *Syriac*.
2. *Hebrew*.
3. *Arabic*.

The Hebrew was intermediate between the other two in its geographical position and its character.

The *Hebrew*, as a language, received its name from the Hebrew people, who were so called for one of two reasons ; the word עִבְרִי is derived either (a) from עֵבֶר, meaning *beyond*, and applied to one belonging to the region beyond the Euphrates eastward, and hence applicable to Abraham, Gen. 14: 13. This derivation has the sanction of the Septuagint, which renders the word ὁ περάτης, which means *the one beyond*. (b) It may be derived from EBER, (Gen. 11 : 14,) an ancestor of Abraham of the sixth generation. (Eber in English has no aspiration, but the loss of the aspirate only shows the transition from Hebrew to English.) Gen. 10 : 25 may suggest the reason why *Eber* was the name given to his descendants. In this passage Eber called his son *Peleg*, because in his days the earth was divided. *Eber* then would be the head of a family after the confusion of tongues, and his descendants would naturally have his name. It is according to *O. T.* analogy that a race should be named from an individual : e. g., Israelites, Ammonites, &c. Whichever derivation be approved, the term *Hebrew* might be expected to embrace other races than the Israelites, and there is such an intimation in Num. 24 : 24. *Eber* is spoken of as a name extending over a number of peoples east of the Euphrates. It has been claimed that Gen. 10: 21, shows that the words " all the children of *Eber*" indicate that the word *Hebrew* came from this derivation. This is not conclusive, because *Eber* may have been the name of a territory. In ordinary language, the term *Hebrew* is used exclusively of the Israelites. Abraham was a Hebrew, but the children of *Keturah*, or *Ishmael*, or *Esau*, were never called Hebrews. *Hebrew* was their *national* name, *Israel* was their *domestic* and *theocratic* name.

From the reign of David, the name *Hebrew* is almost lost, and Israel came to be used for the *ten*

tribes in distinction from Judah. In the *N. T.* the word *Jew* denoted any one belonging to the Jewish people anywhere ; *Hebrews* were those Jews who dwelt in Palestine and spoke the Aramaic. Those who spoke Greek were called *Grecians*, not *Greeks*. The *Hebrew language* is not so called in the *O. T.*, but is called the Jew's language. Isaiah 36 : 11. In Is. 19 : 18, it is called the language of Canaan. The first application of the name Hebrew to a language is found in the Prologue to *Ecclesiasticus*. In the N. T. and Josephus, the term "Hebrew language" is used both for the Hebrew proper and for Aramæan ; i. e., the tongue spoken by the Hebrew people at that time. Jno. 5 : 2 ; Acts 21 : 40. Later Jewish writers called the Hebrew the "*holy* tongue," in distinction from the Aramæan, which succeeded it and was called the "*profane* tongue."

The very high antiquity of the Hebrew is shown from the antiquity of its literature, which is more ancient than that of any other language. The writings of Moses preserve antediluvian fragments ;— e. g., that of Lamech. In these and in proper names, we have glimpses of roots and phrases already obsolete in the time of Moses. The *Targum* on Gen. 11 : 1, says that the Hebrew was the primitive language of the world. Some modern Christian scholars have supported this view for the following reasons :—

1. That the proper names from Adam to Babel are derived from *Hebrew* and have a Hebrew meaning.

2. The fragments from Lamech and Noah are certainly Hebrew.

3. The great longevity of the Patriarchs, which was such that Adam was contemporaneous with Methusaleh, and he with Shem, and Shem with

Abraham. Thus Adam is joined to Abraham by two links or generations.

4. It is not probable that the pious people took part at Babel. Some say that the race of Shem were not there, and that hence their language was not confused and therefore not destroyed. This reasoning, however, is not conclusive, for it assumes that these proper names and fragments have been preserved, not only as to their exact *signification*, but in their original *form*, and have neither been translated nor explained in reference to Hebrew etymology. To all this we say :—(1) The names which are undeniably foreign to the *Hebrew* may often admit of a satisfactory Hebrew explanation ; e. g., in Ex. 2 : 10, " Moses" is an Egyptian name, (meaning " drawn out of the water,") but may be explained from the Hebrew. So also *Pharaoh*, (meaning " ruler ;") Ham, as in Ps. 105 : 23 ; Behemoth, (a Coptic word) in Job. 40 ; 15, means "hippopotamus." In Gen. 41 : 43, the word translated " bow the knee" (SHESH) is an Egyptian word, yet may be explained by Hebrew etymology. But it would not do to say that the *Hebrew* was the language of *Egypt*. (2) Proper names are often translated from their original languages into another language ; e. g., ON (a city) is, in Jer. 43 : 13, called Bethshemesh, the " house of the sun," in Greek Heliopolis. So also NO-AMMON is called Διόσπολις, the " city of Jupiter." So Erasmus, Melancthon, Luther, etc., are Greek translations of their own names from their native languages. (3) Some of the names before the confusion at Babel cannot be thus explained ;—e. g., Tubal-Cain, Arphaxad. (4) Such antediluvian words may have been *appellatives* and not proper names ;—e. g., *Adam* (meaning " man,") is connected with אֲדָמָה the ground ; *Eve* is "*life*," *Abel* is " *breath ;*" *Cain* is " possession" and " *weapon ;*" Noah is " *rest.*"

Ezekiel

We need not conclude from these that the Hebrew was the original language of mankind. No language can lay claim to that honor.

Renan, in his history of the Semitic language, says, " since more than a thousand years B. C., the Shemitic roots have suffered no decay or injury. We are dealing with a language of steel, and not with a worm-eaten one. The Shemitic language has preserved to us traces of the primitive tongue." He says that " the grammatical structure savors of the infancy of the human intellect. The radicals of the modern Arabic correspond with the Hebrew. If in 3000 years there was no sensible alteration, can we not conclude that the primitive language was similar to the Hebrew?" It is not impossible that this may be true.

Scientific Philology may one day accord to the Hebrew the honor of being the original language. The Hebrew leaves evidence of being the language of Palestine because their word for *West* was YAM, which is the same as their word for *sea*.

Some have supposed that they were idolaters, because they used the plural אלהים. This is unfounded. It is simply the plural of majesty. *Abraham* came from *Aram* and therefore spoke Aramæan. In Deut. 26 : 5, *Syrian* is used for *Aramæan*. In Gen. 31 : 47, the members of Abraham's family still continued to speak *Aramæan*.

Is the Hebrew language throughout, of indistinguishable character or diversified like others?

1. The differences are due to diversities of " dialects."
2. They are due to the *different species of composition*.
3. Differences also arise from *successive periods of time*.

We will consider them in order.

1. Differences due to *Dialects*.

Some have gone to a great length in dividing up the dialects of the Hebrew. A recent German writer gives three dialects. (1) That of *Ephraim* on the North ; (2) of *Judah* in the middle, (3) of *Simeon* on the South. More sober critics say we have no data for this, because the small extent of Palestine and the frequent assemblies of the people would prevent the formation of such dialects. There were undoubtedly provincialisms, as there are now in the United States. E. g., in Judges 12 : 6 ; Neh. 13 : 24. In Judges 18 : 3, the Danites are said to have known the voice of the Levite by his dialect. This not so. They simply recognized it as the voice of an acquaintance.

In the N. T., (Matt. 26 : 73) we read that Gallileans could be distinguished by their speech.

2. The differences in *composition* are wider.

The lang. of *poetry* and *prose* differs much in all languages. Poetry delights in rare and unprosaic and bold forms of speech. E. g., (1) Rare words:—

דָּבָר, word, כְּלָה אִמְרָה אֹמֶר
בּוֹא, to go or come, אָתָה
אִישׁ, man, אֱנוֹשׁ גֶּבֶר
עָשָׂה, to do, פָּעַל
נָטַע, to plant, שָׁתַל
לֹא, not, בַּל
קְרָב, war, = מִלְחָמָה
זָהָב, gold, = כֶּתֶם

(2,) Words used in a different sense in poetry. Attributives often substituted for nouns. Ex.:

שֶׁמֶשׁ, sun, חַמָּה, hot.
יָרֵחַ, moon, _ לְבָנָה, white or pale.
נוֹזְלִים (*flowing*), used poetically for *streams*.
אָבִיר (*mighty*), " " " God.

(3.) Peculiar *grammatical forms* for the same word.

אֱלֹהִים = אֱלוֹהַּ, God.

יָמִים = יְמוֹת, days.

שָׁנִים = שְׁנוֹת, years.

עֲמָמִים = עַמִּים, nations (by resolution of the Daghesh-forte.)

יֵלֵךְ = יַהֲלֹךְ, will go, (taking the form הָלֹךְ in the future.)

בְּ, from, = בְּנֵי   יַעֲלֵי or יֵעָל   אֱלֵי or יַעֲלֵי

The suffix ךָ   כִּי   עֲדֵי - עַד   בְּ   בְּמוֹ   כְּ - כְּמוֹ

(4.) Some peculiar *endings* or *terminations*.

ה, = ת,   יְ = ים   כוּ - ם   יַכוּ - יַהֶם

יְ, = יהוּ or וֹהִי   יָ   כִּי

(5) Peculiar grammatical constructions. The demonstrative זוֹ (or poetical וּ) used for the relative אֲשֶׁר. The relative often omitted, also the article. Bold ellipses.

Many of these forms are called Arabisms or Aramæisms and said to be borrowed from the Aramæan. But this is not so. They seem to belong to that common stock of all the Semitic tongues from which the Hebrew and Aramæan and the Arabic all came. In the Hebrew these terms passed into disuse and were used only in poetry, while they were retained in the Aramæan or Arabic.

The book of Isaiah is almost all poetry, Daniel almost all prose. The Prophetic style occupies an intermediate place between poetry and prose. In the books of Moses we find both poetry and prose. In Deut., we find the prophetic style.

3. Differences arising from *successive* periods of time.

The Hebrew language underwent a great change between the beginning and end of the Old Testament. The most obvious division is into *two* periods.

The point of separation between these was shortly before the Babylonian exile.

(1) From the time of Moses to the time of Isaiah the language suffered little change. In the writings of the later prophets, (Jeremiah, Zephaniah, etc.,) there is a manifest decline, produced by a large influx of foreign words, especially Aramæan. The Jews were brought into contact with these nations. Esther, Daniel, Ezekiel, Nehemiah, and Ezra, exhibit a striking contrast in purity. The Book of Chronicles was written later than Kings, and hence is more corrupt. Ezekiel shows the greatest number of varieties in form and the greatest variety of anomalies, which exhibit an actual deterioration of the languages. In the prophets subsequent to the exile, Haggai, Zechariah and Malachi, the language is less corrupt, and there is an advance to the former purity and correctness of style. The stationary character of the language during the former period, (there being no change for 800 years,) is made the ground of an objection to the antiquity of the Pentateuch. To this we reply

(a) that it is the character of all of the *Semitic* languages to be fixed and stationary. All the customs and habits and even the names of places, are unchanging, in some cases the names being the same now as in the time of Abraham and Joshua. The Syriac and Arabic also have the same permanence. Chinese scholars say that the writings of Confucius (550 B. C.,) do not differ in language from the best writers of the present time in China.

(b) The circumstances favored this preservation of language, (α) because they had little intercourse with other languages, separation being required by their laws ; and (β) the Canaanites also spoke the *Semitic* language.

(c) The books of Moses containing the civil and religious code served to *fix* the language, as the *Koran* has the Arabic, and Luther's Bible the *German*, and the English Bible the *English*. They also furnished a model of writing, as *Homer* did to the *Greeks*. The language of Moses would often be better fixed, even after the spoken language had itself changed.

(d) The Hebrew was not wholly stationary during this long period. There are some changes; e. g., the third feminine pronoun הוא in the Books of Moses is changed to היא in Isaiah; נַעַר is used in the Pentateuch to denote either a boy or girl,—in Isaiah it was used with the *feminine* ending נַעֲרָה for a girl. The Plural is used for both always. Some words and phrases are peculiar to the Pentateuch and never occur afterwards; others vanish until the later writings of the O. T.; others, which Moses used in prose, occur again later only in poetry. In I. Sam. 9 : 9, mention is made of a change in a word, viz., *seer* as changed to *prophet*. Some say that in Exodus 6 : 3, God revealed a new name of Himself to Moses. This was not a new name, but was meant to show a new phase of his character.

(2.) Many new words and phrases, and a more frequent use of vowel letters, i. e., "*scriptio plena*," as distinguished from "*scriptio defecta*," appear in the later books, and also the adoption of genuine Aramaisms.

Examples of new phrases : כִּכְלָבָה with the plural construct later ; מִלְכוֹת ; לֶחֶם הַפָּנִים, bread of the presence, shew bread, is in later books לֶחֶם הַמַּעֲרֶכֶת (from מַעֲרֶכֶת a row, עָרַךְ, to arrange). God of Heaven, is later hovah of Hosts.

Thus the *decay* of the Hebrew is not always distinguishable from *poetic license*. For this reason the character of the Hebrew in any book is not a criterion of its date or age.

Did the *written* Hebrew differ from the *spoken?* It may have to some extent, as in Eng. The latest books of the O. T. represent a purer style than could have been current among the people at that time, and was formed from a careful study of the ancient models.

When did the Hebrew cease to be *spoken?* 1. The Talmud and the Jewish grammarians and some Christian scholars say that the Hebrew was displaced by the *Aramæan* at the time of the Babylonish exile, though it long continued to be known by the old men who had learned it in Palestine, and also by the learned men. The young generation spoke Aramæan and knew nothing of the Hebrew. 2. It is thought by some modern scholars that the Hebrew, though corrupted by the exile, continued to be the language for 400 years after the exile, that is, until the Maccabees and the Syrian domination. These advocates are influenced mainly by the hypothesis that some of the books of the O. T. were written during this period. Heh. 13 : 24 is no proof that the *Hebrew* was unchanged as a *spoken* language. Is. 36 : 11 does not prove that the Jews still spoke *Hebrew ;* nor, on the other hand, does Neh. 8 : 8 prove that they had given up Hebrew and adopted Aramæan. They say that the passage shows that the Levites *translated* the book of the law ; this is not so, but our version is correct, where we read that they read the law " distinctly," with explanations. And a captivity of only 70 years was too brief a time for them to give up their own language and adopt another, especially as only a part of the people were carried away, and the remainder were not put among Aramæans. The Prophets too, in the later books, after the exile, would not have used a language unknown to the people. The deterioration of the language began before the exile, though it was accelerated by that exile. The Chaldee was famliar, as seen from Daniel and Ezra.

The change was a *gradual* transformation. We cannot tell the exact date of the change any more than we can tell that of the Anglo-Saxon into English, or of the Latin into Italic. But it could not have been long after the exile.

CHARACTER OF THE HEBREW.

There are no adequate data for estimating or ascertaining the copiousness of the Hebrew language. Gesenius gives 5642 words in the Hebrew Bible, with about 500 roots. But these are only those found in the O. T., and hence are not the entire vocabulary of the language.

Shultans, living in the last century, calculated the number of the combinations of the letters of the alphabet into triliteral roots, finding 12000 of them, and to each of these he assigned 30 derivates; hence he makes 360,000 words, not reckoning quadriliterals and their derivatives.

This principle is false. The number of words in any language does not depend on the number of roots, nor upon the number of possible combinations. The stock of words will not go beyond the necessities of a people. Ideas and objects unknown would of course have no words. Simple agricultural peoples, like the Hebrews, knowing little of the outside world, and uniform in their modes of life, would not have a very extensive circle of ideas, and hence of words. Yet the language shows an affluence of synonyms. E. g., there were eight terms for *darkness*, seven names for the *lion*, four for the *ox*, eleven for the different kinds of rain. These and other instances show a great richness and profuseness of terms and a careful observation and nicety of distinction between objects and a close study of nature, etc. This quality is favored by the parallelisms of their poetry.

The Hebrew is richest in religious words, e. g., there are fourteen expressions for *confidence in God*, nine for *forgiveness of sins*, twenty-five for the *observance of the Law*.

The structure of the Hebrew language is such as to produce an economy of words and roots. A small number of each do a large amount of service. The paucity of adjectives is compensated for by the distinctions in abstract nouns. The different species of the same verb express different ideas; e. g., *Come* and *bring* are expressed by different species of the same verb; so also to *eat* and to *feed;* to *learn* and to *teach ;* to *go* and to *lead*.

There were also modifications of meaning by the construction of the sentences, e. g., לִרְאוֹת to see, with different forms has different constructions, and with prepositions can mean to *see, look, enjoy, despise, live, choose, provide, visit, learn from, aim at, respect, care for, abide for, know, appear, show, perceive*. Nouns from the same root,—*prophet, vision, mirror, form, sight, vulture* (i. e., keen sight.)

Some lost roots in the Hebrew have left their traces, but can now only be explained by the Arabic. The great number of ἅπαξ λεγομενα suggests that a great number of words have been lost. The Arabic most frequently preserved the primitive grammatical forms, but the Hebrew retained the primary meanings of words the longest. The Arabic has the most verbal simplicity, Hebrew next, Aramæic least. In Hebrew the relics of some independent species

are found, which in the other two languages appear rarely, and as imperfect anomalous forms; e. g., plural endings, paragogic letters, of which the Arabic shows the formation and connection. The primary significations of words are retained in the Hebrew, when in the cognate languages it has given place to a derivative and secondary sense; e. g., מָה in Hebrew always means *what*, though sometimes used as a negative;—in the Arabic, it is a negative. שָׁנָה in Hebrew means *to untie;* in Arabic it means *to dwell*, to put up for the night, (from the idea of untying the beasts of burden. הָיָה to *wander*, in Hebrew; in Arabic and Aramæic means to be *idolaters*, (i. e., to wander in a religious sense.) הָלַךְ =*to go* in Hebrew; in Arabic, *to perish*. שָׁנָה in Hebrew means to *change;* in Arabic and Aramæic means to change *the understanding*, to be mad, deranged. אָמַר to *say*, in Arabic means to say *with authority*, to command (=English *Emir*.) כָּפַר in Hebrew means to *cover;* in Arabic, to cover the truth, to disbelieve. Hence is derived the name of the Kaffir (in Africa,) who does not believe the Koran. An exception is the Hebrew to *miss the mark*, to *sin*, which in Arabic means the former only.

Most words borrowed from the Syriac and other languages are connected with idolatry. The word which in Syriac means to worship, (סָגַד) in Hebrew means to worship idols. Syriac to supplicate, (כָּשַׁף) in Hebrew means to use enchantment. The Syriac for priests, כְּמָרִים, in Hebrew means priests of idols.

The Hebrew contains a very few words not of Shemitic extraction. In the Pentateuch; (1) there are several Egyptian words, especially names of objects, persons, places, e. g., יְאֹר river (always referring to the Nile,) אָחוּ bulrushes, תֵּבָה a box, (=the ark in which Moses was put,) אֵיפָה an ephah, פַּרְעֹה Pharaoh,

אֶבְרֵךְ bend the knee. (2) In the later books there are a few names of Indian objects; there are some Sanscrit words, e. g., ophir, nard, dellian, aloes, ivory, apes, peacocks,—which show the extent of country to which the Phenician navigators had penetrated. In Esther 1 : 6, the word for cotton or linen (כַּרְפַּס) was a Sanscrit word. (3) Persian words were introduced during the Persian rule. In Ezra, Nehemiah, Esther, David, and Chronicles; e. g., Satrap; also names of monarchs and coins, as darix, dram (Ez. 8 : 27.) Xerxes, Cyrus, Haman; also the word for crimson, red of worms, (coming to us through the Arabic.) Pleasure ground פַּרְדֵּס, paradise, in Cant. 4 : 13. (4) There are a few names of musical instruments in Dan. borrowed from the Greek. A number of words are transferred from the Hebrew or Phenician into the Greek and from thence into the Western languages, (a) by Phenicians, (b) by Christians, (c) by modern Jews. Such words are hyssop, balsam, copper, ebony, jasper, alphabet, amen, ephod, hallelujah, cummin, cinnamon, sapphire, seraph, cherub. caballa, jubilee, Sabbath. From the modern Jews we have Rabbi, Sanhedrim, Targum, Mishna. The Hebrew yielded to the Aramæic after the exile, yet both were used and studied by the more learned. The Aramæic became the popular, and the Hebrew the learned language. The Mishna, the oldest portion of the Talmud, is in corrupted Hebrew. The more modern portion of the Talmud is in Aramæic, the dialect of the people. From the 11th Century onward there is a decided tendency to return to the Hebrew. It is still a learned language among Jewish scholars.

I. SHAPE OF THE LETTERS, AND THE ORIGIN OF THE VOWELS OF THE HEBREW LANGUAGE.

All the Hebrew manuscripts which we possess are written in the present square character, but on Jewish coins supposed to belong to the time of the Maccabees, and in the books of the Samaritans, we find a round character similar to the Phenician and Samaritan.

Is, then, the present square character the original one ?

This was a subject of dispute in the 17th century between the Buxtorfs and Capellus. Buxtorf, a Professor at Basle, together with his son and successor, maintained that the square letters were the original ones. Capellus, Professor at Somer, first opposed this view. The Buxtorfs assumed that " there were two separate characters in use, one the *sacred letter* found in the Bible, the other, the secular letter used in business transactions. This latter one is what was found on the coins. During the exile at Babylon, the Priests kept up a knowledge of the sacred writing, but the common secular dialect fell into disuse, while those Jews who were left in Palestine had only the secular character, because they had neglected the reading of the Law, and the Samaritans borrowed their characters from them. When Ezra returned to Palestine, he restored the old sacred character." This hypothesis they supported

1. By the analogy of other nations. The Egyptians had a threefold character. (a) The Hieroglyphic; (b) The Hieratic, or sacred; (c) The Demotic, or popular. The Persians used different methods of writing for history, poetry and letters. The Turks had also a threefold character.

2. From Isaiah 8 : 1. They say that the phrase "a man's pen" refers to the secular, ordinary, or common character.

3. From a passage in Irenæus, who speaks of a Sacerdotal character in use among the Hebrews.

The verse in Isaiah merely means to *write plainly*. Irenæus is really no authority on this subject, because he was ignorant of the Hebrew language, as other mistakes made by him clearly show. The argument from analogy would illustrate the fact if proved, but is no proof in itself. This hypothesis is now abandoned.

Gesenius says that the secular character was that in use by Judah and Israel until the Babylonish Captivity, and then it was preserved by the ten tribes and the Samaritans, while Judah adopted the character of their Babylonian captors, i. e., the square character.

This would account for the early traditions and the inscriptions found at Palmyra. But,

(1) This does not account for the use of the coin letter so late as the time of the Maccabees.

(2) There is no reason to believe that the square letter ever was used at Babylon.

It is now settled that all the Semitic families, as to their alphabets, are related to the old Phenician, which was the original letter, and that from it came that Hebrew character which was used on the coins at the time of the Maccabees. The square character succeeded this slowly and gradually by successive changes through a long period of time. The change was similar to the change in Greek from uncials to cursives. The connecting links between the alphabets we can trace by means of inscriptions at Palmyra and in Egypt. When the change took

place cannot now be determined. It must have been before the 3d or 4th Century, A. D.

Quotations from Origen and Jerome show that the Hebrew character, in their day, was the same as in ours. Jerome says that the word יהוה was read by the Greeks as if it were ΠΙΠΙ. This shows that the square characters were in use at that time. The change probably took place before the time of Christ, as, in Matt. 5 : 18, "*jot*," (i. e., Yodh,) would seem to indicate; for in the old character the ׳ was as large as any of the letters, but in the square character it is the smallest.

If, in examining the Septuagint, it could be found that there had been errors of transcription, such as confounding ר and ד, it would show that the *square* character was used at that time. No satisfactory results, however, have ever been obtained from this examination. We must assume that the change took place between the time of the Maccabees and the time of Christ.

This question has often been mixed up with other questions. It has been treated as if it affected the Bible and its text. Capellus said that the Hebrew text of the O. T. was full of mistakes, and needed constant revision. The Buxtorfs held extreme views in the opposite direction. They said that the text of the Bible had letters of the same shape in which it was given. To say that the Samaritans had kept the old alphabet and that the Jews lost it, seems to be admitting the superiority of the Samaritan over the Heb. Bible. The form of the letters, however, does not affect the purity of the text.

II. This question was subsidiary to another, relating to *the antiquity and authority of the vowels and accents*.

The Rabbins in the middle ages he'd that the vowels were either an integral part of the text, or that they were divinely sanctioned as added by Ezra. Elias Levita held that the vowels were added afterwards by the Jewish grammarians at Tiberias. The elder Buxtorf replied, trying to show that the vowels were not made by grammarians. Levita's arguments found favor with Capellus, who wrote them out and strengthened them, and then sent the MS. to the elder Buxtorf, who commented on it and returned it, confessing the difficulties of the case, and advising him not to publish it. It was printed, however, in 1624, and Buxtorf was expected to reply to it, but did not do so. His son, however, in 1648, published a work which was (1) a refutation of Capellus, and (2) a proof of the antiquity of the vowel-points.

His views were adopted by the orthodox party in Europe and England. It was even made an article of faith in one of the Swiss Confessions of Faith, that the *vowels* and *points* of the Bible were *inspired*. John Owen attacked Capellus, and thought that it would impair the truth of the Bible to believe that such an important matter as the vowels was fixed by unbelievers, and by men who as Jews were under a curse, and were the murderers of Christ. It is now admitted that the vowels are not ancient. We may infer this,

1. Because the minuteness of their notation implies that the Hebrew was not a living tongue when they were introduced.

2. From the analogy of kindred languages. The Syriac and Samaritan have no vowel points, nor did the Phenicians have any, nor were any found on the coins or on the monuments. The Arabic in the Koran has a few vowels, elsewhere none.

3. Tradition among the Rabbins, that the vowels were handed down orally until the time of Ezra, and that he reduced them to writing. They are ascribed to him probably in order that they may have the sanction of inspiration.

4. The Synagogue Rolls, which are greatly esteemed, have no vowels; a fact hard to account for, if vowels formed an original part of the text.

5. The different readings of K'ri and K'thibh all refer to the consonants and not to the vowels. And yet the vowels are much more open to dispute and variation.

6. The present vowel system was not in use at the time of the Septuagint, as proved by its translation of some words in a manner consistent with the consonants, but not with the vowels, as we now have them.

When were they introduced? We notice

(1.) That the Jewish grammarians from the beginning of the 11th century had the points, and did not know but that they had always existed. A table of various readings made in 1034 refers to the vowels and points exclusively, and thus we know that they existed at that time.

(2.) The Septuagint and Josephus do not appear to have them. Origen, in his *Hexapla*, gives a pronunciation which does not agree with the vowel-points. Jerome was probably not acquainted with the present vowel system. By vowels, he meant vowel letters; and by accent, he meant vocal utterance. It is doubtful whether the *Talmud* of the 5th century recognizes them. The *Masora* does contain the names of nearly all the vowels, although the K'ri and K'thibh relate to the consonants. The general conclusion is that the points were introduced by Jewish grammarians between the 5th and 10th centuries.

with the intention of preventing all ambiguity of pronunciation and meaning.

Gesenius sets the time to be between the 6th and 8th centuries. This would bring us to about the time when the Arabic and Syriac vowels were first used. Some now began to give up all authority of the points, as being entirely of human origin. Others went to the opposite extreme. Careful examination gives us a medium ground. The signs are Masoretic, but the sounds are not. There was no Rabbinical trifling with the text, but preserved a rigid accuracy in its pronunciation, besides giving traditional commentary on the text. By careful notation they have given us the sounds just as exact tradition had given those sounds to them. They had good facilities, and were accurate and worthy of our trust.

HISTORY OF THE STUDY OF THE HEBREW. It may be divided into two periods. 1. *Among the Jews.* (a) From the introduction of the *Masoretic* System to the 10th century. (b) From the introduction of the *Grammatical* System in the 10th century to the Reformation. 2. *Among Christians.*

I. *Among the Jews.* Schools were established in Jerusalem as early as the time of Christ, for teaching the Scriptures and Traditions. Such were those of Hillel, Gamaliel, and Shamai. After the destruction of Jerusalem, there were schools also at Tiberias and Babylonia. There was no systematic or scientific study of the language, but an adherence to ancient traditions. The very letters of the Bible were reverenced. Even a letter which happened to be written smaller or larger was retained in the text. Even the number of the letters was known. To these scholars we owe the Masora, which are the notes and the vowels, and the Talmud and their Targums or translations.

Geog of Bible

II. *Among Christians.* The Fathers of the Church, except the Syrian Christians, were mostly ignorant of Hebrew, but Origen in the 3d century and Jerome in the 4th century were Hebrew scholars. In the 10th century the schools were transferred to Spain. There, under Arabic rule, they flourished for a long period. There were schools in Toledo, Barcelona, Grenada, and thus, stimulated by Arab grammarians, Hebrew was studied *grammatically* and *scientifically*. Grammars and Lexicons were written which still exist in MS. in European libraries. Especially noteworthy among these scholars were Kimchi and his two sons. The work of David, the younger son, which he called "Perfection," was that used by the Reformers, and formed the basis of similar works till very lately.

From the time of Jerome till the 16th century, the study of Hebrew was almost entirely neglected by the Christian Church. Charlemagne tried to revive the study of the language, and the Council of Vienna, 1311, voted annuities for professors of Hebrew in Vienna. But the resolution was not carried into effect. Raymond Martini studied Hebrew to use it against the Jews, and Nicholas De Lyra studied it to facilitate the exposition of the Old Testament. The Romish Church distrusted the spirit of the Reformers, but the revival of letters called attention to the Hebrew in spite of this opposition. The Rabbins also were jealous of its popularity, and would not give instruction except at exorbitant prices.

The first Hebrew *Grammar* issued by a Christian was made by Conrad Pelican in 1503. He was a monk at Tubingen, and at that time was only 22 years old. He derived most of his knowledge from a Hebrew Bible, aided by a Latin translation.

John Reuchlin was really the father of Hebrew literature and learning in the Christian Church. He published in 1506 a grammar and dictionary called "Hebrew Rudiments," closely following the plan introduced by Kimchi.

Hebrew, from that time onward, has received marked attention, and when the Church declared the Scriptures in the original the only rule of faith and practice, there was a new incentive to study it.

The methods of study underwent several changes.

I. The *Traditional School*, in which everything was settled by tradition, even as regarded the meanings of words and the construction of sentences, etc. The Buxtorfs were representatives of this school. It was the only practical method in early times. It was partial and one-sided, and neglected other important means. It was too narrow in its views, seeking for information only in Jewish Targums, and not in the Septuagint.

II. The *Comparative School*. The Hebrew was compared with the cognate languages, Arabic and Syriac. The Grammars and Lexicons were a comparison of the various Shemitic dialects. This may be called the *Dutch School*. The best early Grammar was the Heptaglot Grammar and Lexicon of Edmund Castell of Cambridge, in Hebrew, Persian, Aramaic, Arabic, etc. Schultans of Leyden applied his knowledge of Arabic to elucidate the Hebrew. He was the best representative of this school. This school was too one-sided on the other extreme. No regard was paid to the Syriac, nor to Rabbinical authority and tradition, and too much to the Arabic. Hence many imaginary significations are found in their works.

III. The *Idiomatic School* rejected all external helps, and substituted a minute examination of the

Things and race for all

text, context, and parallel passages of the Scriptures themselves. But it also was partial. It said all triliteral roots were originally biliteral, and even tried to give each individual letter of the biliteral a distinct meaning, from the form, etc.

This method led to a more accurate study of the peculiarities of the Hebrew, but was not on the whole a good method. All these schools gave a foundation for

IV. The *Comprehensive School*, including all the former methods. The modern scholars adopt this school. Gesenius is its best representative. His Lexicon, however, is not faultless. There are a few ἅπαξ λεγομενα whose meanings are not known; e. g., the names of some of the unclean beasts in Lev. 11, and some terms used in Is. 3. These may hereafter be explained. They are not important words however.

EARLY VERSIONS.

There are *four* versions of the O. T. which are *ancient* and *immediate*. By an *immediate* version, we mean one made directly from the original and not from any pre-existing versions, which would be a *mediate* version. By an *ancient* version, in a technical sense, is meant one made prior to the Masorites. To be of any *critical* authority, it should be both ancient and immediate. A mediate version may be authority in reference to that from which it was taken. These four versions are:

1. The Greek Septuagint.
2. " Chaldee Targums.
3. " Syrian Peshito.
4. " Latin Vulgate.

Each of these represents the traditions of a particular locality. The Septuagint is that version of the text as held by the Alexandrian Jews. The

Targum—by Jews of Palestine. The Syriac Peshito —by the Oriental Church. The Latin Vulgate—by the Western Church. Two of these, the Syriac Peshito and the Vulgate, include the New Testament, and therefore have a critical authority in regard to it also. The LXX. and the Targum are confined to the Old Testament. Besides these, there are several versions *immediate* in the *N. T.* and *mediate* in the *O. T.*, and hence are of no critical value except in regard to the *N. T.*; e. g., the *Itala* and *Philoxenian Syriac*. Both of these made from the Greek Bible, and hence give the original of the *N. T.*, but not of the *O. T.* Other versions are mediate in both; e. g., the *Anglo-Saxon*, made from the Latin. This would also be called a modern version.

I. THE SEPTUAGINT.

The first language into which the O. T. was translated was the *Greek*, and the Septuagint was the first translation. There is now much doubt and uncertainty as to its origin. According to a letter purporting to have been written by Aristeas to his brother Philocrates (see Smith's Dictionary, p. 2919, Vol. IV.), Ptolemy Philadelphus sent Demetrius Phalereus to Jerusalem to obtain a copy of the Jewish Law for his library. The High Priest Eleazar chose six interpreters from each tribe, seventy-two in all, and sent them with a copy of the Law in letters of gold. These men, by conference and comparison, translated the Bible. Josephus gives the same account.

Other writers say that the interpreters were shut up, two by two, in cells, and made out separate copies, and that all the versions agreed in every letter, when compared. There are differences of opinion about this letter of Aristeas. Some regard it as spurious; other receive it in part, and assume that

Manuscripts { Syriacum
             { Parate

?itacismus?Dei { Manuscripts
               { Versions
               { Quotations
               { Conjectures

the *Pentateuch* was thus prepared, but the rest was added afterwards. The majority of critics reject it altogether. The *historical* and *internal* evidences are against it. The *internal* evidence of the LXX, shows that it was made by Alexandrian Jews, and not by the Jews of Palestine, and that it was not done by one person or at one time. It was called forth by the need of the Greek-speaking Jews, of having a copy for their own use.

The *Pentateuch* was translated *first*, and *Daniel last*, judging from the character of the translation. Ptolemy Philadelphus began to reign 283 B. C. The whole of the O. T. must have been translated before the year 130 B. C., as it is spoken of in the prologue to the Book of Sirach, which was made in that year.

The language is Hellenistic Greek. Different portions of the version are of different character. The Pentateuch is the best, but Daniel was so incorrect, that after the time of Origen it was laid aside, and another by Theodotion was substituted for it, and this is the one we have. Ecclesiastes is slavishly literal, to a disregard of the plainest rules. In Jeremiah, verses and chapters are transposed out of their proper order. The translation, in places, shows great liberty in omission and insertion, the most remarkable instance being the systematic variation and alteration in the chronology of chapters 6 and 11 of Genesis. The Samaritan translation also differs from the Hebrew chronology. This Greek Septuagint version was held in the highest veneration in Alexandria and Palestine. Many held it to be inspired. It was read in the Synagogues of the Greek Jews in Palestine, and was used by Josephus, Philo, the Apostles and the Evangelists. The Christian Fathers received it with the same veneration as the Hebrew Bible. As, in their controversies, the

Christians drew their arguments from the LXX., the Jews gradually fell back on the Hebrew original, and hence began to give up the LXX., and at length despised it.

Mutual recriminations arose between the Jews and Christians, as to who had corrupted the text. A number of new translations arose from either party; e. g., Aquila, Theodotion, and Symmachus. These versions did not attain to ecclesiastical sanction or general use, and hence are only preserved in a fragmentary state.

— Aquila, thought by some to be the same as Onkelos, a Jewish proselyte of Sinope in Pontus, during the second century. His version was slavishly literal, even to the particles; e. g., συν is often inserted (as in Gen. 1:1) where the preposition really belongs to the verb. The idiom of the Greek is violated in order to give an exact rendering.

Theodotion, an Ephesian of the second century. His translation was really a revision of the LXX. His translation of Daniel is used in place of the LXX.'s translation of that book, which was very faulty.

— Symmachus, an Ebionite, translated with great freedom, elegance and purity. (See Smith's Dictionary, page 3379.)

In the course of repeated transcriptions, the text of the LXX. has suffered greatly, until Origen complained that every manuscript contained a distinct text. To remedy this, and to furnish aid to Christians in controversy, Origen undertook the labor of removing the discrepancies by comparing the best MSS., and pointing out their agreement with the original Hebrew and with other Greek versions.

This work was called the *Hexapla*. He spent twenty years on it. It was so called because it had six parallel columns. The first column contained the Hebrew text in Hebrew characters; the second, the Hebrew text in Greek characters, so as to be pronounced more readily; the third contained the version of *Aquila;* the fourth, the version of *Symmachus;* the fifth, that of *Theodotion;* and the sixth, the Septuagint text. Besides these, there were two or three additional columns for different *partial versions*. These supplementary versions are only known from their connection with this Hexapla, and a few citations from them. Their authors are for the most part unknown. They are called *Quinta, Sexta,* and *Septima,* from their respective places in the Hexapla. The author of the *Sexta* was probably a Christian, for in Habbakuk 3 : 18, instead of the phrase "thine anointed," he substitutes "Jesus, thy Christ."

The Hexapla was chiefly exegetical and polemical. The purpose was not so much to bring back the Septuagint to its primitive condition as to adequately represent the original Hebrew. The plan of Origen was, when any words occurred in the Hebrew which were not in the LXX., to insert them from one of the other versions, generally from *Theodotion's*, and these were indicated by an asterisk. If, on the other hand, there were any words in the LXX. which were not found in the Hebrew, he prefixed an obelisk to them to indicate the fact.

In addition to the Hexapla of Origen, mention is made by early writers of a *Tetrapla* and *Octapla*. It is not agreed whether these are distinct works or another name for the Hexapla. The Tetrapla may have been so called (1) as containing the *four* principal versions of the Hexapla, or (2) as being a separate publication of those four versions by themselves without the original.

This work was too cumbrous for general use, and probably was never completely transcribed. It was used chiefly for comparison or for making extracts. After the death of Origen, it was preserved at Cæsarea, and was probably destroyed at the sack of the Saracens. Fragments of it have been collected and published at various times.

These labors of Origen indirectly tended to increase the variations, for transcribers often neglected his marks of variation and so confounded the versions.

Lucian of Antioch and Hesychius of Egypt tried to correct the LXX., but all attempts to find out their readings have been in vain. All we know is that their labors did not give us a uniform text, for Jerome still complained of a great diversity of texts in his day.

The MSS. of to-day are not uniform. A great number of MSS. of the LXX. in the libraries of Europe have been examined. The principal ones are the Codex Alexandrinus in the British Meseum, the Codex Vaticanus in the Vatican Library at Rome, and the Codex Sinaiticus at St. Petersburg. The first portion of the LXX. printed was the Psalter, two editions of which appeared before the entire O. T. was printed in Greek, 1482–1486. The Greek Old and New Testaments were first printed in the *Complutensian Polyglot*, in 1522. During the delay in issuing this edition, the *Aldine*, from Aldus Minutius, appeared in 1518. Both claimed to have followed ancient MSS.

A large number of mediate versions were made from the LXX., the early Fathers being familiar with Greek and not with Hebrew, most commonly translating from the Greek. The oldest Latin version is the *Itala*. The *Syro-Hexaplaric* of the seventh century follows the text of Origen's Hexapla. The *Ethiopic* version of the fourth century, also several

Egyptian versions in the Coptic language, in the third and fourth centuries, the *Armenian* in the early part of the fifth century, the *Georgic* in the sixth century, the *Slavonic* in the ninth, and several *Arabic* and one valuable *Gothic* version by Bishop Ulfilas, in the fourth century, of which the O. T. has perished, and only a portion of the N. T. exists.

The *Critical Value* of the LXX. is variously estimated; some giving it no weight whatever, and others placing it above the Masoretic Hebrew. Morinus affirms the superiority of the LXX., and so also does Capellus, who tried to show that in many instances the readings of the LXX. were preferable to the Hebrew. This was regarded as against the authority of the Hebrew. Some modern critics also prefer the LXX. The majority, however, while valuing it greatly, affirm that the Masoretic text is the best and not to be corrected by the LXX.

II. CHALDEE TARGUMS.

These ancient versions or paraphrases are called Targums from a Chaldee root meaning to *explain*, or *translate*. The word *Dragoman*, still used in the East, is derived from the same root. In Ezra 4: 7, the word is translated *"interpret."* These Targums are paraphrases and not exact versions. The Jewish account of them is, that when the Chaldee became the language of the people, and the Hebrew was no longer intelligible, each synagogue appointed an interpreter, as well as a reader, who should translate into Chaldee the Scriptures as read. For the sake of greater certainty and accuracy these extemporaneous translations were superseded by written versions, called *Targums*. They are distinct works by various authors and at different times, each containing one or more books of the O. T. They are variously reckoned.

There are eleven principal ones, viz., *three* on the Pentateuch, *Onkelos, Pseudo-Jonathan,* and the *Jerusalem ; two* on the Prophets, *Jonathan Ben-Uzziel,* and the *Jerusalem ; one* on the Hagiographa by *Joseph the Blind,* containing Job, Psalms, and Proverbs; *one* on the five small books called *Megilloth,* viz., [Canticles, Ruth, Lamentations, Esther, Ecclesiastes ; *three* on *Esther; one* on *I.* and *II. Chronicles.*

The most ancient and valuable is that on the Pentateuch, by Onkelos, and that on the Prophets, by Jonathan Ben-Uzziel. These two are distinguished from all the rest by the purity of their Chaldee, which approaches that of Daniel and Ezra. They are free from the legends of the later Targums, and from arbitrary additions, although Jonathan followed the original less closely(the original) than Onkelos. These two are highly esteemed by the Jews. Onkelos refers Gen. 49 : 10 and Num. 24 : 17 to the Messiah; Jonathan refers Isaiah 53 to the Messiah; According to Jewish tradition, they were both pupils of Hillel, a distinguished teacher of Jerusalem, who died 60 B. C. The accounts are obscure, Onkelos being by some confounded with Aquila.

The Targum of Pseudo-Jonathan on the Pentateuch was so called because it was erroneously ascribed to the Jonathan above mentioned, whereas its barbarous Chaldee and historical allusions assign it to the seventh century.

The Jerusalem Targum is so called either from the place where it was made, or from the dialect in which it was written. It is not complete. It frequently corresponds with the Pseudo-Jonathan. It is doubtful whether it is original, or a compilation from other Targums.

The remainder of the Targums are of comparatively modern date, written in wretched Chaldee,

and utterly worthless for purposes of criticism. There are no Targums on Daniel, Ezra, and Nehemiah. The Talmud says that Daniel reveals the exact time of the Messiah's advent, and therefore should not be made known to the people. The most probable reason was that these books were written in inspired Chaldee, and they were unwilling to mingle with it their uninspired Chaldee.

III. THE SYRIAC VERSION.

This was likewise written in the Aramaic tongue. The *Peshito*, or Old Syriac. It was called *Peshito*, or "*Simple*," (1,) either because of its literal character as a translation, or (2,) because of its plain, unadorned, and simple style, or (3,) because it clings to the literal interpretation, as opposed to the allegorical. It is evidently the work of a Christian translator, perhaps a converted Jew, inasmuch as this was made directly from the Hebrew, and with great accuracy. Most of the ancient versions are made from the LXX. The age of this old Syriac version is disputed, and its origin obscure. It is the basis of the Christian literature of the old Syrian church. It was known in the fourth century, for Ephraim Syrus, who died A. D. 378, makes it the basis of his commentary; and says that it was in common use in the Syrian church. It has been ascribed to the third, second, and even to the first century, prepared during the lifetime of the Apostles themselves. It is urged in favor of its age that it was generally received in the time of Ephraim (Syrus,) and that many words and phrases were at that time obscure, and besides, the early Syrian church would require such a version. On the other hand, it is not supposable that it could have existed more than a century before any other Christian writings appeared in that language. This originally contained only the Canonical books. The

Apocryphal books were afterwards added. It continued to be the received translation among them until the controversy between the Monophysites and the Nestorians gave rise to another.

Paul, Bishop of Tela, made the Syro-Hexaplaric version from the Septuagint of Origen's Hexapla, early in the seventh century; English translation of it by Dr. Murdoch of New Haven.

IV. LATIN VERSIONS.

From a statement made by Augustine, there must have been several Latin versions. He says that those who translated into Greek from the Hebrew could be numbered, but the Latin translators could in no manner be counted. He speaks of one of them under the name of the *Itala*. To this he gives preference on account of its superior accuracy and perspicuity. All these Latin versions were made, not from the Hebrew, but from the Greek,—from the LXX. in the Old Testament, and from the original Greek in the New. This variety of translations produced such confusion and so many discrepancies, that it was complained that there were almost as many different texts as there were MSS.

Repeated solicitations were accordingly made of Jerome, a monk of Palestine, the most learned man of his time, equally skilled in Hebrew, Greek, and Latin, that he should undertake the revision and correction of the Latin versions. In 382 or 383 A. D., at the urgent request of Dámasus, Bishop of Rome, he began a hasty revision of the Gospels, then proceeded to the rest of the N. T., and then passed to the Psalms, and reviewed them afterward more carefully. The first of these two revisions of the Psalms by Jerome was adopted at Rome and hence was called the *Roman Psalter*. The second was adopted in Gaul and hence was called the *Gallic*

Psalter. Jerome, after going over many books of the O. T., then resolved upon a new and independent version from the original Hebrew. He obtained at considerable expense the assistance of native Jews, and made use also of pre-existing Greek versions. Such was the veneration for the LXX. that every departure from it was regarded as a deviation from the word of God and offensive to Him. Even Augustine begged him to desist. Jerome persevered, nevertheless, but kept as closely to the LXX. as possible, sometimes against his better judgment. He began in 385, but the work was not completed and published until 405. Some parts were hastily prepared. He speaks of translating a thousand verses in one day and says that he translated Proverbs, Ecclesiastes, and Canticles, in three days.

This translation is one of the best preserved to us from antiquity. It was long in coming into general use. The old *Itala* continued to be used in connection with it until about the beginning of the seventh century, when all the Western Church accepted it, but retained the old version of the Psalter.

The modern Vulgate consists of the Apocrypha from the Itala, the Psalter of the Itala corrected by Jerome, and the rest is Jerome's version. The Itala and Vulgate have been corrected by each other, and hence both have become corrupted. Repeated attempts have been made by later scholars to correct the text of the Latin Bible. The learned Alcuin in the ninth century, under the direction of Charlemagne, undertook the restoration of the true text.— Also Lanfranc, archbishop of Canterbury in eleventh century and Cardinal Michaelis of the twelfth century. There were several works in the twelfth and thirteenth centuries called the " Correctoria Biblica or Epanorthica," containing also different readings, especially the Sorbonne Edition and that of Hugo St. Clair.

Great importance was given to this Latin version by a decision of the Council of Trent. On the 8th of April 1546, it was decreed that the Vulgate should be held as authentic in public reading, preaching and exposition, and that no one should dare or presume to reject it on any pretense whatever. This decree accordingly contained an order for the printing of an accurate edition. A standard edition was published in 1590 under the direction of Pope Sixtus V., called the Sixtine edition. This was declared to be the one pronounced authentic by the Council of Trent, and the printing of any other copy different from this was forbidden under penalty of excommunication. Errors were immediately discovered in it, however, and only two years after, Clement VIII. published a new edition differing from the other in some thousands of places, and this last is now the standard edition of the Vulgate. This action of the Popes has always been a sore point with those who hold the doctrine of the Papal Infallibility.

Hebrew Manuscripts.

The MSS. of the original in the N. T. are more numerous and older than of the O. T., but this is compensated for by the fact that in the MSS. of O. T. there is greater care and accuracy in transcription. The variations are few and unimportant.

The existing Hebrew MSS. consist of *two* classes:—1. Those for the use of the Synagogue; 2. Those used by private persons. Of the latter there are two classes:—(a) Those written in the *square* letter, and (b) those written in the abbreviated *Rabbinical* letter or running hand.

1. The *Synagogue MSS.* These are the most valuable, and contain those portions of the O. T. which were selected for reading in the Synagogues; i. e., the *Law* and the *Prophets.*

(a) The Law was on *one MS.* The lessons from the Law were read in course, and were called *Parashoth.*

(b) The Prophets were not read in course, but from lessons, and these were written on separate MSS., called *Haphtheroth*, and were numbered to correspond to the passages of the Pentateuch to be read on the same Sabbath. The tradition is that the lessons were originally only to be read from the Law, but when Antiochus Epiphanes forbade the reading of the Law in the Synagogue, lessons were selected from the Prophets to evade the requirement of the king. There were separate rolls for the five smaller books, i. e., the *Megilloth*, viz., Esther, Ecclesiastes, Canticles, Ruth, and Lamentations. Esther was read at the feast of *Purim.* These MSS. or rolls were prepared with the greatest care, according to rules given in the Talmud, which were superstitiously minute. They must be written on parchment prepared from the skin of a clean animal. The text was to be the square character, written in columns, without vowels or points, and to be written in black ink. All large and small letters were to be carefully noted. The copyist must look at each word in the original before transcribing it. The copy must be corrected within thirty days, and if four errors were discovered on one skin, that MS. must be rejected.

These MSS. are very valuable, and are highly prized. Very few of them are in the hands of Christians, because the Jews generally burned them when they became old, lest they should be polluted by the touch of a Christian.

II. *Private MSS.* These are rarely complete. They generally contain only parts of the O. T. Sometimes are written in rolls, but generally bound in books of various sizes.

(a) Those which were written in the *square* character are most valuable, and contain the points and vowels. The letters were written first, the points and vowels being added afterwards. One wrote the consonants, another the vowels and the *K'ri*. Another corrected it. Another added the Masora and Scholia. They are nearly all written in black ink, with ornamented words or letters in the opening paragraphs. The prose was written in columns, and the poetry in clauses. Sometimes the Hebrew text was accompanied by translations in Chaldee or Arabic. The *upper* and *lower* margins contain the Great Masora or traditions as to the text; the *outer* margin the *scholia* or some *Rabbinical* commentary; the *inner* margin the K'ri and Little Masora. Sometimes the material was parchment, but oftener linen or cotton paper.

(b) The Private MSS. in the *Rabbinical* character are mostly on paper, without points, accents, or Masora, and with many abbreviations.

Those MSS. designed for the use of the Synagogues are the most important. The Private MSS. in the *square* characters are next in value, and the Private MSS. in the Rabbinical character are least important.

The determination of the *age* of Hebrew MSS. is very difficult, especially if there be no date or inscription. A criterion available in Greek or Latin MSS., drawn from the shape of the letters, is not available here, because the square letter is the same in all existing MSS. Some MSS. have subscriptions giving the date, but some of these are found to be

fraudulent and are added to increase the value. There is great difficulty in interpreting these subscriptions even when the date is given, because they bear record from different eras, and it is uncertain what these eras were.

The Hebrew MSS. are obtained from the remotest countries, from the Jews in India and China, and have the same text as in our Bibles. A large number of MSS. have been described and examined by Pinner and others. Pinner gives an account of several Hebrew MSS. found at Odessa, which must be by several centuries the oldest known to exist, if his word can be taken. What he regards as the oldest, is the Pentateuch Roll on leather, which was brought to Odessa from Dhagistan. The subscription says that it was corrected in 580, hence it is probably much older than that. Another was written in 843, another in 881.

The oldest MSS. in DeRosse's collection were some rescued from the Genesa at Lucca, where the Jews were accustomed to bury their MSS. These consisted of fragments of the Pentateuch which he supposed to belong to MSS. of the eighth century. The oldest in Kennecott's collection bears the date 1018 A. D.

No uniform Hebrew text is preserved in the Samaritan letters and among the Samaritans, though they have the Hebrew Pentateuch. There is what is called a *Samaritan Pentateuch*, and there is a *Samaritan Version of the Pentateuch*. The first is the Hebrew Pentateuch written in Samaritan letters, by Joseph Skaliger of the sixteenth century. The first copy ever seen in Europe was obtained by Peter Delaval on his return from Palestine in 1662, when he published an account of the countries visited.

The Samaritans now consist of a few families in Nablous. They seem to have lived in small communities at that time. Delaval was in Damascus in 1616, and succeeded in purchasing two manuscripts, one containing the Hebrew text, or the Samaritan Pentateuch, on parchment, which he deposited in a Paris Library; the other, the Samaritan Version of the Pentateuch, he retained himself.

Since this time, various other copies of the Samaritan Pentateuch have been obtained by European scholars. The opinions of scholars vary as to its value. Its first publisher, Morinus, vindicated the claim of the Samaritan Pentateuch to be superior to the Masoretic text; others depreciate it. The strife continued a long time, but the matter is now very much at rest as to the main points. It was claimed by Morinus to have been derived from the Pentateuchs of the ten tribes at the time of the schism of Jeroboam; the common opinion now, however, is that it appeared after the Babylonish exile. Manassas, brother of the high-priest at Jerusalem, being threatened with exclusion from the priesthood for marrying a Samaritan woman, fled to the temple on Mt. Gerizim, carrying the Pentateuch with him, and the modern Samaritan copies are derived from this.

In favor of that view that gives the greatest antiquity to it, it was argued that the hatred between the Samaritans and Jews was such that they would not adopt their books. It was further urged that the Samaritans received of all the books of the O. T. only the Pentateuch. It was urged that, if these were in existence when they borrowed the Pentateuch, they would have taken them likewise. In reply to this, however, we may say that the Samaritans are not the legitimate descendants of the ten tribes, but

are rather the descendants of the heathen colonists introduced by the king of Assyria, after the ten tribes were carried into captivity. The enmity between the two was not a bar to their adopting the books. The Samaritans claimed at the end of the captivity, to be the children of Israel, and offered to unite with them in rebuilding the temple. The Jews refused this claim, which refusal was the basis of the hostility between them. They renewed their claim as often as it was to their interest to do so. This claim was the ground of their hatred. Hence the Samaritans would catch with eagerness anything tending to strengthen their claim. Almost every thing they had was borrowed from the Jews. So they coveted the Pentateuch. Their reverence for the Pentateuch, while rejecting the rest of the O. T., cannot be accounted for by saying this was not written, for other portions were in existence at that time. The Samaritans have a book of Joshua, but not the correct one. The true reason arose out of the nature of their religious system. It was the same as that which led the heretics of the early Christian Church to reject the epistles of Paul, &c. The contents did not suit their creed. The grand Article of Faith with the Samaritans, was, that on Mt. Gerizim everybody should worship, and not at Jerusalem. The Pentateuch was altered for this purpose in more than one place. And all those books which speak of a local seat of God's house after the people were settled in Canaan, were rejected by them from the canon ; but Moses they could not reject. The opinion that it was derived at the schism of Jeroboam has been given up for the reasons given. The period of the defection of Manassas, is the best that can be obtained.

While the Samaritan and the Jewish Pentateuch agree in the main, yet they differ in several thousand readings. A large portion consists merely of the insertion of vowel letters, or the insertion or omission of the copulative conjunction or the article, or other trifling variations. Quite a number, however, are of greater consequence. In upwards of a thousand readings it agrees with the Septuagint as against the Masoretic text. The manuscripts are written with little care and exhibit many discrepancies among themselves. These are of no critical value; yet they agree in many particulars. The investigations of Gesenius have shown that the great body were intentional alterations of the text, made for the purpose of simplifying, etc., the reasons for which can still be assigned. Gesenius gives several classes.

1. Grammatical emendations; unusual forms changed for the more ordinary; archaisms avoided ; want of agreement between verb and subject, noun and adj., etc., in very many cases agreeing with the K'ri.

2. System of explanatory glosses; difficult words or unusual forms of speech explained ; some simpler phrase or word used without varying the sense.

3. Conjectural emendation of a letter or two, to improve the sense and to remove imaginary difficulties.

4. Alterations for the sake of conforming to parallel passages ; e. g., the father-in-law of Moses, in Ex. 4 : 18, is said to be Jether, which the Samaritans make Jethro. The name of Moses' successor, which the Bible occasionally gives in a different way, the Samaritan Pentateuch gives as Joshua. In the genealogies, Gen. 11, "and he died" is added to the name of every patriarch, as in the fifth chap. When-

ever *any* names of the Canaanitish tribes occur, the Samaritan Pentateuch gives *all* of them.

5. The fifth class of corrections involve still greater interpolation, where whole sentences, and often verses, are interpolated.

6. Corrections to remove historical and other difficulties. Ex. 12: 40, "430 years." The Samaritan copy makes this cover the wandering of the Patriarchs in Canaan as well as their settlement in Egypt, by inserting "who dwelt in the land of Canaan." The most remarkable variations occur in Gen. 5 and 11. The Samaritan and the Septuagint text differ here from the Hebrew and from each other. It is easy to discover that both were altered from the Hebrew, but with different ends in view.

7. "Samaritanisms," as Gesenius calls them. In these they slide into their native idioms.

8. Those which have been altered to conform to Samaritan ideas. The removal of anthropomorphisms,—the imputing to God that which belongs to man, e. g., such as would impute bodily passions or human parts to God. Deut. 27: 4.

The Samaritans change Ebal to Gerizim.

The MSS. of the Samaritan Pentateuch were partly on parchment, or on cotton and linen paper; no vowels or pointing; sometimes there is a diacritical line to separate words similarly written; words are separated by a point or by two points.

Three native versions have been made from the Samaritan Pentateuch, one into Greek, one into the Samaritan language, and the third into the Arabic. The last two are still extant. The Greek has perished. These versions are of no account.

CRITICISM AND HISTORY OF THE TEXT OF THE OLD
TESTAMENT.

By text is meant the very words of the writer. The office of criticism is to remove errors in the existing MSS. by means of all the evidence existing. The name criticism is repugnant to some minds from the erroneous notion entertained of it. The legitimate aim of criticism is the restoration of the text as it came from the hands of the sacred penman. It does not produce uncertainty. It establishes the correctness of the received text.

The sources of textual criticism are four-fold. 1. Manuscripts. 2. Versions. 3. Quotations. 4. Conjectures.

1. Manuscripts are liable to error in transcription. If it were not for this they would be certain evidence. These errors are by accident or design.

(1.) *Errors by accident.* Liability to error was greater formerly than now. Yet even now errata are common in printed books. They increase in arithmetical progression in the old manuscripts. There are, (a) errors of the eye. (b) Errors of the ear, one reading while another writes. (c) Errors of memory, causing transposition, omission, interchange, taking parallel passages, etc. (d) Errors of judgment. The erroneous divisions of words ; misunderstanding abbreviations, mistaking syllables for words, and marginal remarks for part of the text. (2.) *Errors by design.* The early Christians charged the Jews and heretics with intentional errors ; with regard to the former they were groundless. Manuscripts were subjected to intentional alterations, made to introduce corrections, etc. This was done designedly, though with good motives; yet it was no less a mistake.

The first consideration in determining the authenticity of a manuscript is its date; another, the care with which it was written, whether there are marks of carelessness; again, the general agreement of the text with other valuable manuscripts.

2. The second class of critical authorities are the ancient versions. By their <u>critical</u> value is meant the aid they give in restoring or settling the true text of Scripture; <u>their hermeneutical</u> value. They place before us the system of interpretation adopted by the translators. To these may be added the <u>exegetical</u> value of a version, the aid which they render us. Now different versions are of unequal merit in these various respects.

These two uses are quite independent of each other. No version can have critical value unless it is both <u>ancient</u> and <u>immediate</u>; the older the better: the nearer the fountain-head, the purer the stream. Those before the Masorites are called *ancient*. Since that time the text is the same as we have before us.

Some have even proposed to substitute a version for the original. So the Council of Trent did in regard to the Vulgate, which they declared authentic. None shall reject it. Some doctors of the Romish Church understand this to legitimatize its use; others understand it to set aside other copies in favor of this. We cannot make the stream higher than its source. No one is willing to rely upon translations, if he can read the original.

None can vie with the original Scriptures as being universally received and authoritative. No one has ever claimed the Vulgate to be inspired. (1) The only gronnds would be that the original has become hopelessly corrupt, or (2) wholly unintelligible. For the first, it must be shown that this corruption did not enter before the version was made.

As to the second, it must be shown that the version has been kept pure itself. It has been shown that the original Scriptures have been preserved purer than any other. And that it is unintelligible without points, which are of human authority.

This argument is at fault both in the premises and in the conclusion. The Hebrew Bible can be read without the points. Ancient and valuable translations may be used as helps, but not substituted in its place. This argument has been abandoned by the greater number.

Versions are not of as great importance as manuscripts. If a copy is taken from a manuscript and one from a version, the version would be one step from the source. Manuscripts, therefore, are the primary authorities in criticisms, versions of secondary authority. No new reading on the sole authority of versions should be admitted, though they may lend their aid. It is necessary to institute careful examinations of the versions, separately. The first inquiry must be as to the state of the version itself. The work of the version depends upon the accuracy of the copy from which it is made.

Versions have another source of corruption peculiar to themselves, viz., the interpretation and correction of one version from another. When the primary text of the immediate versions has been obtained, the question arises, does it give a free or literal translation? If free, it is of little worth to the critic. Further, if it gives a paraphrase, it increases the hermeneutical value, but ruins it for critical purposes. For the aid of the critic, it is better if it renders every particle, however unintelligible it might be made.

Closely allied with the preceding is the nature of the language into which the version was made.

The closer the affinity between the languages, the clearer the meaning, and the less the change. A version into Syriac would have an advantage over one into the Greek or the Latin.

Another point is the general accuracy of the versions, including the fidelity and ability of the translators. The use of a version in the criticism of the original requires great caution.

3. Third source of criticism is quotations found in the early writers. The first printed editions known to have been taken from ancient manuscripts since lost are entitled to credit, corresponding to their respective sources. Some internal grounds arising from these various readings themselves. The most general rule is, *that reading which will give the most satisfactory account of all the others is probably the true one.* For this reason the most difficult reading is often to be regarded as the original one. Yet this rule must be used with caution. Again, *that reading which gives the best sense, and agrees best with the text ;* the *style of the author* also may furnish a presumption in favor of one reading. An improper use has often been made of parallel passages. Copies sometimes give parallel passages instead of the true one. It is particularly so with the Psalms. Discrepancies are often proof of the conscientious care with which they are preserved.

4. Where everything else fails, recourse must be had to critical *conjecture.* Our object should be to determine what the text actually was, not to determine what it might have been. Our authorities are so ample that critical conjecture is only to be resorted to in extreme cases, or not at all. This is much more extensively used in the profane writings. *maud*

The general result of all this is to establish the correctness of the inspired text. None of them materially affect the inspired text. While the mechanical correctness of the text is maintained, its correctness in the main is established. There could have been no mutilations before the time of the Saviour, for He or the Apostles would have exposed them. They charge the Jews with other sins, but not with this. To this agrees their own scrupulous adherence to the word of God, and their superstitious veneration for it. It has not been changed since the time of the Saviour, from the impossibility of Jews combining to corrupt them, scattered as they are over the world. Then they had no access to those in the hands of the Christians.

The internal evidence of their Scriptures is the same as the Christians have. The charges of this nature made by the early Christians seem to have arisen from the veneration in which the Septuagint was then held. While the Jews were guiltless of wilful alteration, they took great pains to prevent errors, which are almost unavoidable in repeated transcriptions. Even the size of the letters, position of the letters, finals and medials, etc., were transmitted from age to age, and so printed in our Hebrew Bible. Guarding it thus, they counted the verses, words, and even the letters of Scripture, marking the middle word, etc., showing the disposition to preserve them entire.

The mass of criticism called the Masora accumulated gradually; the beginning was very early. It is now very unweildy. There are the Great Masora and the Little Masora; the latter is an abridgement of the former. To the Masora belong the K'ri and the K'thibh, (*read* and *written*,) referring exclusively to the letters, never to the vowels. They are about one thousand in number. The origin of these various readings is involved in great uncertainty.

Perhaps from the collation of MSS. It seems plain that all did not arise from this source. Many arose perhaps from a desire for grammatical uniformity. K'thibh refers to the original text, the K'ri is a gloss upon it. The K'thibh and K'ri do not stand side by side as resting upon independent authority. The K'thibh was placed in the text, and required it to be read according to the K'ri in the margin. This seems to show that the Masora found already in existence a text which was to be considered true and unaltered. They made no alterations in the context.

The first portion of the Hebrew Bible ever printed was the Psalms, in 1477, accompanied by a commentary. The Hebrew Bible was printed entire at St. Senna in the duchy of Milan, in 1488 ; only nine copies of this are known to be in existence. The second complete edition, the one which Luther used, was made six years later. Luther used it in making his German Bible. By a Rabbinical Bible is meant a Hebrew Bible containing the Chaldee Targums as well as the Masora and the commentaries of the Rabbins. Three editions have been printed ; Daniel Vombar in 1518, Buxstorf in 1618 (a copy of which is in the Seminary Library,) Amsterdam in 1724.

The text of the Pentateuch was divided for reading in the Synagogue into 54 sections ; these were subdivided into 669 lesser divisions, called *Parashoth*. These smaller sections are some of them designated by the פ or ס. The large sections are marked with three large פ's or ס's ; corresponding are the lessons from the Prophets, the *Hafturas*. When the reading of the Law was prohibited, the reading of the Prophets took its place. Chapters are of Christian origin. Cardinal Hugo first introduced them into the Vulgate in the 13th Century. The division of the Bible into verses is as old as the system of accents. *(u.*

By a critical edition we mean one having a collection of various readings. The most noted are those of How, begun in Paris in 1753; and of Kennicott in Oxford in 1776. This last is made from 694 MSS. De Rosse, a few years later, exhibited various readings from 700 MSS. The Polyglot exhibits several ancient versions possessing critical authority. There are four principal Polyglots; Complutensian - Polyglot of Spain, Antwerp, Paris, and London. A copy of each is in the Seminary Library. The Antwerp edition, or " Biblia Regia," in 8 Vols., 1569, was published under the patronage of Philip of Spain. The Parisian is in 10 Vols., 1645, and was published at Paris. The London Polyglot in 6 Vols., folio, in 1657.

www.ingramcontent.com/pod-product-compliance
Lightning Source LLC
Chambersburg PA
CBHW022006220426
43663CB00007B/979